Soul Fuel

BMW R NINE T

Customizers

TEXTS BY
DIRK MANGARTZ

teNeues

BLITZ
MOTORCYCLES
Independent
Custom Garage
GoRide
Blacksmi
Records

Foreword by Michael Lichter

It was 1978 and I was a week late for the 38th annual Sturgis Rally. I just finished getting my V-Twin together after some light customization and headed straight to the Black Hills. When I arrived, there wasn't a bike on the street in sight, so I kept on going—north to Canada, around the Great Lakes, past Niagara Falls ... My trip became an adventure with lots of breakdowns, serendipitous encounters and great people all the way to New York City. Every bolt that could have shaken loose on the old iron did, but it didn't matter—it was all part of the experience. When I was out riding back then, I photographed the world around me. At 22, I started going to more bike events and photographing the people, bikes, and fun I witnessed. My images made it into *Easyriders Magazine* and assignments followed. I quit my restaurant job, told the be-bop band I played drums with my sticks were being hung up, and miraculously, 40 years later, I'm still photographing custom bikes and the biker scene and still loving it, only now it's for books and magazines around the globe. Photography became my livelihood. It became my life.

In the '70s, when car doors were nervously locked beside you at red lights, bikers were all thought to be outlaws. As the years passed, bikers came to be accepted to the point where it became cool to ride, so of course, everyone wanted in. Like myself, a number of the other campers from the early Sturgis days became part of a business that grew around custom bike culture. By the 2000s, when custom biking burst onto television, the business exploded. The times were fat so front ends got longer, engines bigger, wheels taller and skins became more elaborate, that is, until 2008, when many businesses went down in flames with the economic crash. As things turned out, the ashes were like fertilizer to a quietly flourishing movement that had been growing slowly. Young riders wanted to make their bikes more personal and more fun to ride. They wanted simpler bikes, more adventure and escape from their parents' woes. As Dirk Mangartz outlines so well in his introduction, around the world, this new generation brought new passion and a new way of seeing things to the world of motorcycling. Ola Stenegard bore witness to how the crash threw accelerant on the movement and how slow growth became fast change. He understood what was needed at exactly the right time with the Concept Ninety prototype from BMW's design team and Roland Sands. Not only did BMW bring an easy to modify platform to the table with the R nineT, the company's respect for individual creativity and passion led them to the amazing Soul Fuel project chronicled here in this book. These 17 customs helped change how bike enthusiasts viewed BMW and offered a model for Japanese, American, and other European brands to follow.

Zur 38. Auflage der jährlich stattfindenden Sturgis-Rallye kam ich eine Woche zu spät. Es war 1978 und ich hatte meinen Zweizylinder-V-Motor nach einer kleineren Überarbeitung gerade wieder zusammengesetzt. Anschließend machte ich mich auf den Weg in die Black Hills, aber als ich ankam, war kein einziges Motorrad mehr auf der Straße. Also fuhr ich weiter, nordwärts Richtung Kanada, um die Großen Seen herum und an den Niagarfällen vorbei. Die Tour wurde zu einem Abenteuer mit vielen Pannen, großartigen Menschen und Zufallsbegegnungen auf dem Weg nach New York City. An meiner alten Maschine löste sich jede Schraube, die sich nur lösen konnte, aber das gehörte einfach mit zum Erlebnis. Unterwegs fotografierte ich die Welt um mich herum. Als ich 22 war, besuchte ich noch mehr Motorradveranstaltungen und hielt dabei die Menschen, die Motorräder und die Stimmung fotografisch fest. Meine Bilder wurden in der Zeitschrift *Easyriders* veröffentlicht, weitere Aufträge folgten. Ich gab meinen Job im Restaurant auf und verließ die Bebop-Band, in der ich Schlagzeug gespielt hatte. Es mag wie ein Wunder erscheinen, aber 40 Jahre später fotografiere ich immer noch umgebaute Motorräder und die Bikerszene, jetzt aber für Bücher und Zeitschriften in aller Welt, und ich habe immer noch großen Spaß daran. Die Fotografie sichert nicht nur meinen Lebensunterhalt, sie ist mein Leben.

In den 1970ern, als die Leute ihre Autotüren verriegelten, wenn man an der roten Ampel neben ihnen hielt, wurden Biker durch die Bank für Gesetzlose gehalten. Im Laufe der Jahre hat sich die Wahrnehmung jedoch geändert: Motorradfahren gilt mittlerweile als cool und jeder möchte Teil der Bikerkultur werden. Ebenso wie ich haben sich viele andere Enthusiasten, die Sturgis in früherer Zeit erlebt haben, in der Geschäftswelt etabliert, die rund um Custombikes entstanden ist. Als das Umbauen von Motorrädern in den 2000ern im Fernsehen populär wurde, erlebte dieses Geschäft explosionsartiges Wachstum. Es waren fette Zeiten, in denen die Vorbauten länger, die Motoren stärker, die Räder größer und die Gestaltung der Oberflächen ausgefeilter wurden – zumindest bis 2008, als viele Unternehmen während der Wirtschaftskrise zu Asche zerfielen. Es stellte sich aber heraus, dass diese Asche einen guten Dünger für eine langsam erblühende Bewegung abgab. Junge Menschen wollten ihre Motorräder persönlicher gestalten und mehr Spaß beim Fahren haben. Sie sehnten sich nach einfacheren Maschinen, mehr Abenteuer und der Flucht vor den Sorgen der Eltern. Wie Dirk Mangartz es in seiner Einleitung so schön beschreibt, erweiterte diese neue Generation die Welt der Motorräder um neue Leidenschaft und eine neue Sichtweise. Ola Stenegard war dabei, als der Crash diese Bewegung beschleunigte und aus dem langsamen Wachstum ein rascher Wandel wurde.

Rudi
Sturgis, SD. 1988

Mit dem Prototyp Concept Ninety vom BMW Konstruktionsteam und Roland Sands bewies er, dass er erkannt hatte, was zu diesem Zeitpunkt nötig war. BMW hat nicht nur die R nineT als eine leicht abzuwandelnde Plattform ins Spiel gebracht. Angetrieben vom Respekt für Kreativität und leidenschaftliches Engagement hat das Unternehmen auch das faszinierende Projekt Soul Fuel gestartet. Dieses Buch stellt die 17 Custombikes vor, die bis 2018 unter dem Label Soul Fuel entstanden sind. Sie haben das Bild verändert, das sich Motorradbegeisterte von BMW machen, und ein Vorbild für japanische, amerikanische und europäische Marken geschaffen.

The most compelling aspect of this book with its stories of passionate builders and their innovative Soul Fuel creations is how they demonstrate the energy and excitement of these times. Not that it wasn't a blast 40 years ago, but as far as I'm concerned, the level of creativity and talent today exceeds anything I ever saw before, so much so that I can unequivocally say this is absolutely the best time to be involved with custom motorcycles. And this is just the beginning!

Es macht dieses Buch mit seinen Geschichten leidenschaftlicher Bastler und ihrer innovativen Kreationen so unwiderstehlich, dass es die Energie und Spannung der aktuellen Customszene fühlbar macht. Das soll nicht heißen, dass es vor 40 Jahren nicht auch schon toll war. Aber die Kreativität und das Talent, die sich hier zeigen, übersteigen alles, was ich je zuvor gesehen habe. Deshalb kann ich uneingeschränkt sagen, dass wir gerade die beste Zeit des Customizings erleben. Und dabei ist dies erst der Anfang!

Michael Lichter has photographed the world of custom bikes and biker culture since the 1970s. His work appears in magazines around the world and he has 11 coffee table books to his credit (and and has contributed to many more). He exhibits his own personal photography widely and since 2000, he curates and produces a large annual themed custom motorcycle art exhibition at a 7,000 sq. ft. gallery at the Sturgis Buffalo Chip where he tirelessly works each year to introduce new customizers and moto-artists to the media and custom bike world (including 3 of these Soul Fuel customizers with their R nineT creations.)

Michael Lichter fotografiert Custombikes und die Bikerkultur seit den 1970er Jahren. Seine Arbeiten erscheinen weltweit in Zeitschriften und werden in Ausstellungen gezeigt. Er hat bereits elf Bildbände veröffentlicht und zu vielen weiteren beigetragen. Seit 2000 zeichnet er als Kurator und Produzent für eine umfangreiche Kunstausstellung über Custombikes in einer Galerie im Sturgis Buffalo Chip verantwortlich, wo er den Medien und der Bikerwelt jedes Jahr neue aufregende Bastler vorstellen möchte. Darunter waren bislang auch drei Soul Fuel Customizer mit ihren Interpretationen der R nineT.

02

The Customizing Way of Life

Fingers
GASKETS

SOUL FUEL
NEXT GENERATION CUSTOM MOTORCYCLES

The customizing movement ran out of steam at the tail end of the 1990s. Customized motorcycles mutated into ever busier caricatures of their chopper ancestors. Extremely wide tires inspired reckless riding. Extensive on-board electronics and an enormous amount of billet aluminum led to a gaudy, nouveau riche appearance and made the bikes prohibitively expensive for the average person. How did this come about? *Easy Rider*, released in 1969, changed the motorcycle world with a movement towards freedom, adventure, and rejection of bourgeois middle-class values. Choppers were the ultimate expression of the zeitgeist. Stretched motorcycles with seemingly endless forks, footpegs shifted right forwards and a stepped bench seat were considered expressions of individuality. Riding a chopper was a clear political statement against the conventional and narrow-minded establishment. The subculture's scene organized itself into biker clubs, while motorcycle conversion specialists and an active accessories industry gained a foothold. Bikers and their choppers were cool. Not only in the United States, but in old-world Europe as well.

By the beginning of the twenty-first century, however, the attraction of converted motorcycles and the corresponding scene had dried up. Hippie anarchy and rock god aspirations had become outdated in the face of the demands and desires of the digitized world. The champions of the earlier customizing movement had also grown old and tired. Strict club hierarchies, romanticized campfire nostalgia and a timeworn *Born to be Wild* soundtrack did not have the power to draw in new followers. The customizing scene continued to limp along without bringing anything new to the table, much less expanding its base.

However, the magic that customized motorcycles emanate should not be underestimated. Shortly after the dawn of the new millennium, the seed of an entirely new scene began to blossom in Europe. Several international bike builders simply ignored the craft's traditional values, which were steeped in the idea that modifications were primarily just for American bikes in a chopper or dragster style. They put motorcycles from all manufacturers—cheap Japanese bikes from the 1970s, full-bodied Italian bikes or classic BMW Boxers—on their workbenches and rebuilt them however they wanted to. They made reference to nearly forgotten styles like sporty cafe racers,

SOUL FUEL
NEXT GENERATION CUSTOM MOTORCYCLES

Eigentlich ist das Thema Customizing Ende der 1990er-Jahre gegessen. Motorradumbauten mutieren zu immer aufwendiger gestalteten Karikaturen ihrer Chopper-Urahnen. Extreme Breitreifen sorgen für ein fragwürdiges Fahrverhalten. Umfangreiche Bordelektronik und reichhaltig verbautes Billet-Aluminiumzubehör wirken nicht nur neureich, sie stellen den Durchschnittsverdiener auch vor eine echte finanzielle Herausforderung. Doch wie war es dazu gekommen? Unter dem Einfluss des Roadmovies *Easy Rider* von 1969, dem Drang nach Freiheit, Abenteuer und der Abkehr von den bürgerlichen Werten der Mittelschicht hatte sich die Motorradwelt verändert. Chopper waren das Ding jener Zeit. Lang gestreckte Motorräder mit beinahe endlosen Gabeln, vorverlegten Fußrasten und Stufensitzbank galten als Ausdruck von Individualität. Mit einem Chopper traf man eine klare politische Aussage gegen das spießige Establishment. In Bikerclubs organisierte sich die subkulturelle Szene, Spezialisten zum Umbauen der Motorräder und eine rührige Zubehörindustrie etablierten sich. Biker und ihre Chopper waren cool. Nicht nur in den USA, sondern auch im alten Europa.

Spätestens Anfang des neuen Jahrtausends jedoch verflüchtigt sich der Reiz umgebauter Motorräder und der dazugehörigen Szene. Hippie-Autarkie und Rockerehre bilden Ansprüche und Wünsche der digitalisierten Welt nicht mehr ab. Zudem sind die Protagonisten der frühen Customizing-Bewegung alt und müde geworden. Weder strenge Club-Hierarchien noch Lagerfeuerromantik und beharrlich gedudelter *Born to be Wild*-Sound haben die Kraft, Nachwuchs zu rekrutieren. So dümpelt die Customszene weiter vor sich hin, ohne jedoch echte Impulse zu setzen oder gar neue Kreise zu erobern.

Aber niemand sollte die Magie unterschätzen, die von individuell umgebauten Motorrädern ausgeht. Schon kurz nach der Jahrtausendwende sprießt in Europa das zarte Pflänzchen einer völlig neuen Szene. Einige internationale Bike-Builder scheren sich nicht um die überlieferten Werte, nach denen vorrangig US-Bikes im Chopper- oder Drag-Style modifiziert werden. Sie stellen Motorräder aller Hersteller – preiswerte Japaner aus den Siebzigern, kernige Italiener oder klassische BMW Boxer – auf ihre Werkbänke und bauen sie nach eigenen Vorstellungen um. Sie orientieren sich an beinahe vergessenen Stilen wie den sportlichen Cafe Racern, den Scramblern als

scramblers as precursors to enduros, bobbers from the '40s, or flat track racers from the United States. Combined with original, fresh ideas and eyes open to the spheres of modern life, an entirely new scene has emerged.

The new trend has spread across the world like wildfire. Workshops tailored to certain subcultures are popping up in the coastal metropolises of the United States, in Japan and Australia, in the major cities of Spain, Italy, and in the remote areas of Scandinavia. In many cases, these workshops are owned by figures from the creative scene instead of typical mechanics or tinkerers. More than a few have worked as photographers or in advertising. In their work, they bring along a corresponding professionalism to the scene.

The motorcycles they design share a common philosophy of a reduction to the essentials. Aesthetic, lightweight, streamlined, and purist bikes in an extremely wide range of manifestations were soon being ridden through the capital cities of Europe and over the mountainous regions of North America. Though usefulness and suitability for a given purpose often take a back seat to personal style, these converted bikes are perfectly suitable for daily use without any limitations on function. "There's nothing worse than a show bike that you can't ride," says customizer Jens vom Brauck based in Cologne, Germany. Neither high engine output nor high-tech components play a very important role. Fun is necessary; creativity is encouraged.

For some new-generation custom bike owners and builders, opposing the overly complicated digital world plays a key role. The bikes are purposely kept simple so that anyone can tinker around with them whenever they feel like it without becoming overwhelmed. Thankfully, there is a pure, unadulterated, authentic riding experience out there. There is also a widespread longing for a counterpoint to a world that is changing at hyperspeed. Legendary BBC Radio DJ John Peel summarized this by saying nonchalantly, "Somebody was trying to tell me that CDs are better than vinyl because they don't have any surface noise. I said, 'Listen mate, life has surface noise.'" Accordingly, a younger audience is discovering the daring appeal of these bold, yet simple two-wheelers. Before, this demographic rejected a motorcycling world that included safety vests, fold-down visor helmets, and super tourers. Now it's succumbing to the charm of good style. And what do you know—motorcycles have regained some of their rebelliousness!

Vorläufer der Enduros, den Bobbern der 1940er-Jahre oder den Flat-Track-Rennmaschinen aus den USA. In Kombination mit eigenen, frischen Ideen und wachsamen Blicken auf die moderne Lebenswelt bildet sich eine völlig neue Szene.

Der neue Trend verbreitet sich wie ein Lauffeuer über die gesamte Welt. In den Küstenmetropolen der USA, in Japan und Australien, in den großen Städten Spaniens, Italiens oder der Weite Skandinaviens: Überall entstehen subkulturell geprägte Workshops. Oftmals sind die Besitzer dieser Werkstätten keine klassischen Schrauber oder Mechaniker, sondern stammen aus der Kreativszene. Einige haben bislang als Fotografen oder Werber gearbeitet. Entsprechend professionell können sie ihre Arbeit in Szene setzen.

Die daraus resultierenden Motorräder eint der gemeinsame Gedanke von der konsequenten Reduktion aufs Wesentliche. Ästhetische, leichte, schlanke und puristische Bikes in unterschiedlichsten Ausprägungen fahren schon bald durch europäische Hauptstädte oder amerikanische Bergregionen. Obwohl oft Zweckmäßigkeit und Nutzen dem persönlichen Stil untergeordnet werden, sind die umgebauten Bikes voll alltagstauglich und uneingeschränkt funktionstüchtig. „Es gibt nichts Schlimmeres als Showbikes, die unfahrbar sind", bringt es der Kölner Customizer Jens vom Brauck auf den Punkt. Dabei spielen weder hohe Motorleistung noch Hightech Komponenten eine wichtige Rolle. Spaß soll es machen, kreativ darf es sein.

Für manchen Erbauer oder Besitzer eines Custombikes der neuen Generation spielt auch die Abkehr von der komplizierten digitalen Welt eine entscheidende Rolle. Denn an den bewusst simpel gehaltenen Bikes kann jeder nach Lust und Laune schrauben, ohne sich maßlos zu überfordern. Zum Dank gibt es ein unverfälschtes, pures und gefühlsechtes Fahrvergnügen. Der legendäre BBC-Radiomoderator John Peel bringt den Wunsch nach einem Gegenpol zur sich immer schneller drehenden Welt nonchalant auf den Punkt: „Jemand wollte mir erzählen, CDs seien besser als Vinyl, weil sie keine Störgeräusche haben. Ich habe gesagt: Mann, das Leben hat Störgeräusche." So entdeckt auch eine jüngere Zielgruppe den Reiz der simplen und frechen Zweiräder für sich. Fühlten sie sich von Warnwesten, Klapphelmen und Supertourern bislang eher abgeschreckt, erliegen sie nun dem Charme des guten Stils. Und endlich, so scheint es, haben Motorräder wieder etwas Rebellisches!

THE MAGIC THAT CUSTOMIZED MOTORCYCLES EMANATE SHOULD NOT BE UNDER-ESTIMATED.

NIEMAND SOLLTE DIE MAGIE UNTERSCHÄTZEN, DIE VON INDIVI-DUELL UMGEBAUTEN MASCHINEN AUSGEHT.

Twenty and thirtysomethings with flannel shirts, full, well-groomed beards, and stylishly streamlined motorcycles flock to events such as Wheels and Waves, which has been held in Biarritz, France every year since 2012. Visitors to the festivals, mostly young and hip, drink craft beer, explore the sandy beach with their bikes, and are finally giving a face to the modern motorcycle world again. Wheels and Waves is considered the linchpin of a new motorcycle culture, while other gatherings such as Pure and Crafted in Berlin or Born Free in California are following suit. The motorcycle industry is quick to notice the trend towards custom bikes. BMW Motorrad was one of the first manufacturers to consider offering a motorcycle specifically geared to the new market. In 2005, a small team headed by former Chief Designer Ola Stenegard, Head of Design Edgar Heinrich and Project Manager Roland Stocker put all their talent and dedication into developing a heritage bike. The goal was to create a pure roadster that is easy to customize and has a classic, dynamic appearance. Stenegard has been an eagle-eyed observer of the eclectic motorcycle scene. "All of a sudden, people are interested in motorcycles again. Sometimes it feels like the return of *On Any Sunday* or *Easy Rider*. It is one of these elemental moments of history that unleashes a genuine enthusiasm for motorcycles. For those of us who work in the motorcycle industry, these moments are the most inspiring."

BMW Motorrad Designer Torsten Dauner, who sadly died much too young in 2007, drafted initial sketches and models of the concept study, which went under the moniker BCC (BMW Custom Concept) in the early days. Even at this early stage, it was

Youngster mit Flanellhemd, akkurat gezupftem Vollbart und stilsicher abgespeckten Motorrädern strömen zu den angesagten Veranstaltungen wie dem Wheels and Waves, das seit 2012 in Biarritz stattfindet. Die meist jungen, modebewussten Besucher chillen, nippen am Craft Beer, driften mit ihren Bikes am Sandstrand und geben der modernen Motorradwelt endlich wieder ein Gesicht. Das Wheels and Waves gilt als Fixpunkt einer neuen Motorradkultur, andere Treffen wie Pure and Crafted in Berlin oder Born Free in Kalifornien folgen schon bald. Schnell bemerkt auch die Motorradindustrie den Trend zu Custombikes. Als einer der ersten Hersteller macht sich BMW Motorrad Gedanken über ein passendes Fahrzeug für den neuen Markt. 2005 begibt sich ein kleines Team um Ola Stenegard, Ex-Chef Fahrzeugdesign, Head of Design Edgar Heinrich sowie Projektleiter Roland Stocker mit viel Herzblut an die Entwicklung eines Heritage-Bikes. Das Ziel: ein purer Roadster, der sich einfach individualisieren lässt und über ein klassisch-dynamisches Erscheinungsbild verfügt. Ola Stenegard hat die heterogene Motorradszene genau beobachtet: „Auf einmal interessieren sich die Leute wieder für Motorräder. Manchmal fühlt es sich an, wie die Rückkehr von *On Any Sunday* oder *Easy Rider*. Es ist einer dieser elementaren Augenblicke der Geschichte, die eine wahre Motorradbegeisterung entfachen. Für uns, die wir in der Motorradindustrie arbeiten, sind dies die inspirierendsten Momente."

Der 2007 viel zu früh verstorbene BMW Motorrad Designer Torsten Dauner fertigt erste Skizzen und Modelle der zunächst BCC (BMW Custom Concept) getauften Konzeptstudie an. Schon in diesem Stadium wird deutlich, wie wandlungsfähig ein

clear how versatile a prospective new heritage bike can be. The bike is planned as a sporty cafe racer, as a roadster with a one-person saddle and as a bobber. Each one of these different versions firmly takes aim at the senses of the beholder. German biker magazine *Motorrad* cannot stop talking about the first blueprints: "Boom! One glance is a mind-blowing experience that just keeps going. Flickering on the retina, making alarms ring out in your brain. A motorcycle that is all lean muscle, stripped of all fat ... a reduction to the bare essentials." The effusive praise continues. "The BCC can't be pigeonholed. It is neither a cruiser nor a cafe racer, nor a traditional naked bike—but has a little bit of everything in its DNA."

Based on a BMW HP2 Megamoto, the hardworking team fabricates an initial 1:1 model. The developers model the gas tank from synthetic materials, with two ellipsoid headlamps stacked one above the other, serving as the front headlight. This study makes clear just how seriously the designers and technicians took the requirements brief in order to make the bike suitable for customizing. A claim underscored by an upside-down fork instead of the Telelever front wheel guide typical of other BMW models, the screwed-on rear frame and, not least, a cable harness that allows for the replacement of electric components like headlights or indicators.

Once Hendrik von Kuenheim, who headed BMW Motorrad from 2008 to 2012, greenlit the project, preparations for series production began. In 2008, the project and the studies that followed it were renamed Custom Concept. The project group decided to switch out the HP2 frame for a newly developed tube arrangement that is less complex and offers space for a voluminous aluminum tank. Instead of the new liquid-cooled boxer engine, the engineers stuck with the air-cooled 1200 power plant for the BMW, now christened R nineT. A solid 110 HP instead of a bubbly 125 HP was the perfect choice for the purist roadster.

In the searing heat of the Spanish Sierra Nevada, a select group congregated. The BMW bosses, a camera crew and a handful of invited designers were on hand. Initial test rides were carried out to awaken enthusiasm for the R nineT and to provide a basis to discuss collaboration with the international bike community. At the end of a long day, the decision was made to send R nineTs to selected customizers from around the world so that they could present their vision of a stand-alone motorcycle. Even before the R nineT appeared in dealer showrooms, BMW Motorrad gave four

künftiges New Heritage-Bike sein kann. Geplant ist es als sportlicher Cafe Racer, als Roadster mit kurzem Einmannsattel oder als Bobber. Und jede dieser unterschiedlichen Versionen zielt mit aller Macht auf die Sinne des Betrachters. Die Zeitschrift *Motorrad* lässt ihrer Begeisterung über die ersten Entwürfe freien Lauf: „Bumm! Bereits der erste Blick lässt reihenweise Synapsen platzen. Flimmern auf der Netzhaut, Alarm unter der Schädeldecke. Ein Motorrad gebaut bloß aus Muskeln, ganz ohne Fett ... Reduktion aufs wirklich Wesentliche." Und weiter: „Die BCC entzieht sich Schubladendenken, passt in keine herkömmliche Motorradkategorie, ist weder Cruiser noch Cafe Racer noch traditionelles Naked Bike, trägt aber von allen Gene in sich."

Auf Basis einer BMW HP2 Megamoto fertigt das engagierte Team ein erstes 1:1-Modell. Den Benzintank modellieren die Entwickler aus Kunststoff, als Frontleuchte dienen zwei übereinander angeordnete Ellipsoidscheinwerfer. An dieser Studie wird deutlich, wie ernsthaft sich die Designer und Techniker eine „Eignung zum Umbauen" ins Lastenheft geschrieben haben. Eine Upside-down-Gabel statt der bei anderen BMW Modellen üblichen Telelever-Vorderradführung, der geschraubte Heckrahmen und nicht zuletzt ein Kabelbaum, der den Austausch elektrischer Komponenten wie Scheinwerfer oder Blinker erlaubt, unterstreichen diesen Anspruch.

Als Hendrik von Kuenheim, BMW Motorrad Chef von 2008 bis 2012, grünes Licht für das Projekt gibt, kann die Vorbereitung für die Serienproduktion beginnen. 2008 werden das Projekt und die nun folgenden Studien in Custom Concept umbenannt. Die Projektgruppe entscheidet sich für den Austausch des HP2-Rahmens gegen ein neu entwickeltes Rohrgeflecht, das weniger komplex ausfällt und zudem Raum für einen voluminösen Alutank bietet. Statt des neuen flüssigkeitsgekühlten Boxeraggregats setzen die Techniker bei der nun R nineT getauften BMW weiter auf das luftgekühlte 1200er-Triebwerk. Kernige 110 PS anstelle wohl gedämpfter 125 PS sind die perfekte Wahl für den puristischen Roadster.

Da stehen sie nun zusammen, bei 30 Grad mitten in der spanischen Sierra Nevada. Die BMW Oberen, ein Filmteam und eine Handvoll geladener Designer. Erste Probefahrten sollen nicht nur die Begeisterung für die R nineT wecken, sondern eine Diskussionsgrundlage für die Zusammenarbeit mit der internationalen Bike Community bilden. Am Ende eines langen Tages ist es beschlossene Sache: Ausgesuchte Customizer aus der ganzen Welt werden R nineTs erhalten, um ihre Vision eines eigenständigen

pre-production models to select bike builders, each of whom built a one-of-a-kind model how they wanted to. Four finished custom bikes—from Roland Sands, Urban Motor, Blitz, and El Solitario—were available on the market the moment the bike went on sale.

The R nineT was initially planned as a short-run series. However, the Bavarians were absolutely overrun by customers on the series launch day in 2013. The waiting list for the new bike was long. Customizers who previously specialized in converting older bikes now wanted to get their hands on the latest BMW. The carefully implemented project from the development department has since become a true success story—and a veritable paradigm shift for the Bavarian company's brand image. The conservative clique of engineers has become a lifestyle studio. Instead of innovative technology made in Germany, the focus is now on coolness and just having fun being alive.

Encouraged by the tremendous success of the new heritage machine, BMW Motorrad resolved to use the numerous communication options it has as an industrial group to give other underground bike builders a chance to take their skills to the big stage. The Soul Fuel project was born. "We value individualists who have a clear philosophy of life—they are our inspiration. We want to share our enthusiasm for them with the whole world," says Thrass Papadimitriou, Head of Business Development for the Heritage project at BMW Motorrad, showing the tremendous respect he has for the customizers' creations. "Craftsmanship is rare in mass production. Custom garages around the world take advantage of their creative freedom by putting a personalized touch on their work and creating unique masterpieces made from metal. BMW Motorrad searched for and found the most talented craftsmen around the globe with the goal of supporting them in exploring their creative ideas. These masterpieces have stirred our souls and fueled our imagination." The models derived from the R nineT, the scrambler and the cafe racer, provided inspiration for the modification pros. Since then, 17 customizers—from the United States, Taiwan, Spain, France, Sweden, and Germany—have realized their ideas of the ultimate one-of-a-kind piece (with many more to come). This book is devoted to these very different 17 Soul Fuel bikes, their visionary builders, and the magic of the new custom scene. Who knows? You might even be inspired with customizing dreams of your very own. Enjoy!

Motorrads präsentieren zu können. Noch bevor die R nineT in den Verkaufsräumen der Händler steht, vergibt BMW Motorrad vier Vorserienmodelle an ausgewählte Bike-Builder, die daraus je ein Unikat nach eigenen Vorstellungen bauen. Bereits zum Verkaufsstart existieren vier fertige Custombikes – von Roland Sands, Urban Motor, Blitz und El Solitario.

Zunächst ist die R nineT als Kleinserie geplant. Doch bereits zum Serienanlauf 2013 werden die Bayern von ihren Kunden regelrecht überrannt. Die Warteliste auf ein Neufahrzeug ist lang. Customizer, die bislang vor allem ältere Motorräder umgebaut hatten, wollen sich jetzt auch an der aktuellen BMW versuchen. Das sorgfältig aufgesetzte Projekt der Entwicklungsabteilung ist zu einer veritablen Erfolgsstory geworden – und leitet ganz nebenbei einen Imagewandel bei der bayerischen Motorradmarke ein. Aus dem konservativen Ingenieurskonzern ist ein Lifestyle-Atelier geworden. Statt innovativer Technik „made in Germany“ stehen Coolness und Spaß am Leben im Vordergrund.

Ermutigt vom großen Erfolg der New Heritage-Maschine beschließt BMW Motorrad als Industriekonzern mit seinen zahlreichen Kommunikationsmöglichkeiten, weiteren Untergrundschraubern eine große Bühne zu verschaffen. Das Projekt Soul Fuel ist geboren. „Wir schätzen Individualisten, die eine klare Lebensphilosophie haben – sie sind unsere Inspiration. Unsere Begeisterung für sie möchten wir mit der ganzen Welt teilen“, blickt Thrass Papadimitriou, Leiter Business Development für das Project Heritage bei BMW Motorrad, mit großem Respekt auf die Werke der Customizer. „In der Massenproduktion kommt Handwerkskunst kaum vor. Custom-Garagen in aller Welt nutzen ihre kreative Freiheit, indem sie ihre DNA auf Serienmotorräder übertragen und einzigartige Meisterwerke aus Metall formen. BMW Motorrad hat talentierte Schrauber gesucht und gefunden, um sie beim Verwirklichen ihrer Ideen zu unterstützen. Ihre Resultate sind Treibstoff für unsere Fantasie.“ Auch von den Derivaten der R nineT – Scrambler und Cafe Racer – lassen sich die Umbauprofis inspirieren. Seither haben 17 Customizer aus den USA, aus Japan, Taiwan, Spanien, Frankreich, Schweden und Deutschland ihre Idee vom ultimativen Einzelstück realisiert (und viele weitere werden folgen). Diesen höchst unterschiedlichen 17 Soul Fuel-Bikes, ihren visionären Erbauern und der Magie der New Custom Scene ist dieses Buch gewidmet. Wir wünschen viel Spaß beim Lesen – und vielleicht auch beim Umsetzen eigener Customizing-Träume.

MOTORCYCLES HAVE
REGAINED SOME OF THEIR
REBELLIOUSNESS!
MOTORRÄDER HABEN
WIEDER ETWAS REBELLI-
SCHES!

03 The Men & The Machines

BMW Motorrad

Roland Sands Design

BMW MOTORRAD
ROLAND SANDS DESIGN
CONCEPT NINETY

CUSTOMIZER	BMW MOTORRAD
ESTABLISHED	1923
LOCATED	MUNICH, GERMANY
INFO	WWW.BMW-MOTORRAD.COM

BMW Motorrad

BMW MOTORRAD & ROLAND SANDS DESIGN CONCEPT NINETY

1973: Motorcycles had a reputation for being wild and rebellious. Year by year, manufacturers were giving them more cylinder capacity and higher power. BMW Motorrad was among those companies who recognized that the era of the dependable long-distance bike was over. The R 90 S, which designer Hans A. Muth had created as a high-end model of the "/6" series, marked a radical upheaval of traditional market values. The motorcycle featured a 67 bhp, 900cc engine and was one of the fastest series motorcycles in the world, reaching speeds of nearly 200 km/h. In addition, it was the first series-production motorcycle to have a cockpit fairing attached to its handlebars, which was made of fiberglass-reinforced plastic. These features were combined with a rear section attached to the seat and flashy colors (the R 90 S series motorcycles were only made in Daytona orange or smoke gray). The Bavarians had created a true icon of the '70s. Never before had a BMW Motorrad designer contributed to developing a motorcycle. Perhaps this is why, out of everything that BMW has designed, the R 90 S remains one of the most treasured collector's items.

No question about it: The company wanted to come up with something unique to celebrate the 90th anniversary of BMW Motorrad and the 40th anniversary of the BMW R 90 S. The goal was to pay homage to a golden era of motorcycles by creating a one-off bike that served as a throwback to the stylistic features of the R 90 S and gave onlookers a direct preview of the upcoming R nineT. The BMW team brought Roland Sands, a former motorcycle racer and popular custom bike designer from California, on board for the project. The son of Perry and Nancy Sands, founders of the motorcycle accessory brand Performance Machine, enjoyed a successful career in motorcycle racing. Soon afterwards (or, in Sands' own words, "32 broken bones

BMW MOTORRAD & ROLAND SANDS DESIGN CONCEPT NINETY

1973: Motorräder galten als wild und rebellisch. Sie erhielten von ihren Herstellern von Jahr zu Jahr mehr Hubraum und Leistung. Auch BMW Motorrad erkannte, dass die Zeit der gutmütigen Langstreckenkräder vorbei war. So bedeutete die R 90 S, die Designer Hans A. Muth als Spitzenmodell der „Strich Sechs"-Baureihe entworfen hatte, einen radikalen Bruch mit den traditionellen Werten der Marke. Die 67 PS-starke 900er zählte mit einer Höchstgeschwindigkeit von knapp 200 km/h zu den schnellsten Serienmotorrädern der Welt; daneben verfügte sie als erste Serienmaschine über eine lenkerfeste Cockpitverkleidung aus glasfaserverstärktem Kunststoff. In Kombination mit einem eleganten Heckbürzel an der Sitzbank und auffälligen Farben – serienmäßig gab es die R 90 S nur in Daytona Orange oder Rauchsilber – kreierten die Bayern eine Ikone der 1970er-Jahre. Nie zuvor hatte ein Designer zur Entwicklung eines BMW Motorrads beigetragen. Vielleicht zählt die R 90 S gerade deshalb heute zu den begehrten Sammlerstücken innerhalb der BMW-Palette.

Keine Frage: Zum 90. Geburtstag von BMW Motorrad und zum 40. Jubiläum der BMW R 90 S wollte sich die Marke etwas ganz Besonderes einfallen lassen. Als Hommage an eine goldene Motorrad-Ära sollte ein Projektbike entstehen, das einerseits die wesentlichen Stilmerkmale des Jubilars zitiert, auf der anderen Seite einen unverhohlenen Ausblick auf die bald erscheinende R nineT gibt. Das BMW Team holte den ehemaligen Motorradrennfahrer und gefragten Custombike-Designer Roland Sands aus Kalifornien ins Boot. Der Sohn von Perry und Nancy Sands, den Gründern der Motorradzubehörmarke Performance Machine, hatte unmittelbar nach seiner erfolgreichen Rennfahrerkarriere (oder wie er selbst sagt: „32 Knochenbrüche später") das eigene Label Roland Sands Design gegründet und mit qualitativ hochwertigen und progressiven

FOR HEAD OF BMW MOTORRAD DESIGN, EDGAR HEINRICH, AND ROLAND SANDS THE CONCEPT NINETY EMBODIES "PURE EMOTION."

EDGAR HEINRICH, LEITER BMW MOTORRAD DESIGN, UND ROLAND SANDS SIND SICH EINIG: DIE CONCEPT NINETY IST EINFACH „EMOTION PUR".

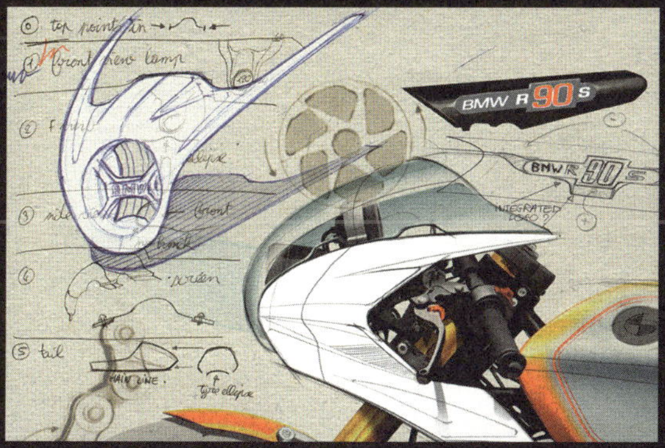

later”), he decided to shake things up by creating his own brand called Roland Sands Design and providing high-quality and forward-looking accessories for custom bikes. Today, Sands is known for his pure motorcycle designs, which are based on a mixture of sports bike and chopper influences. “A carefully crafted, yet still aggressive sense of power with a touch of nostalgia for the bobber,” says the self-made man in an apt description of his own designs. Since the bike builder from Los Alamitos is also a good friend of Ola Stenegard, who was the chief of vehicle design at BMW Motorrad at the time, it only made sense to instigate a collaboration project for the anniversary bike.

The BMW Motorrad design team went to work with plenty of self-confidence. Close collaboration with Roland Sands and careful craftsmanship gave birth to the fairing, tank, seat, and rear section. The creative team continually looked to the historic precedent for inspiration. As a result, the Concept Ninety (as the homage was dubbed) is based on the visual separation of the upper ergonomic and aerodynamic components from the dark-painted motor and chassis section. The technical components have been kept black to symbolize concentrated energy, precision, and high performance. The single-light design is another example of a sporty interpretation of the classic model. However, the Concept Ninety has replaced the H4 round headlight used in past models with modern LED lighting. The chassis parts have been painted in bold ’70s orange as a throwback to the R 90 S. The orange on the front fairing, tank, and rear section contrasts with the elegantly brushed aluminum.

The breathtaking Concept Ninety was unveiled during a special event. BMW Motorrad presented the show bike in front of an audience that assembled at the 2013 Concorso d’Eleganza Villa d’Este, an annual elegance competition for the world’s most exquisite cars and motorcycles taking place near Lake Como in Italy. The extraordinary custom bike inspired tremendous applause from the crowd while giving them an inkling of a project that is still in development: the R nineT.

Accessoires für Custombikes für Furore gesorgt. Heute ist Sands bekannt für seine geradlinigen Motorradentwürfe, denen eine Mixtur aus Sportbike und Einflüssen der Chopperszene zugrunde liegt. „Kultivierte Aggression mit einem Hauch Bobber-Nostalgie“, nennt der Selfmade-Mann seine eigenen Entwürfe treffend. Da der Bike-Builder aus Los Alamitos zudem ein guter Freund des damaligen BMW Motorrad Fahrzeugdesignchefs Ola Stenegard ist, lag der Schritt nahe, für das Jubiläumsbike eine Kooperation zu zünden.

Das BMW Motorrad Designteam ging selbstbewusst an die Arbeit. In enger Zusammenarbeit mit Roland Sands entstanden Verkleidung, Tank, Sitzbank und Heckbereich in sorgfältiger Handarbeit. Die kreative Crew orientierte sich dabei stets am historischen Vorbild. So basiert die Concept Ninety, wie die Hommage getauft wurde, auf der optischen Trennung der oberen Ergonomie- und Aerodynamik-Komponenten vom dunkel lackierten Motor- und Chassisbereich. Die schwarz gehaltenen Technikkomponenten symbolisieren geballte Kraft, Präzision und starke Performance. Auch das Single-Leuchten-Design ist ein Beispiel sportlicher Interpretation des klassischen Vorbilds. Der damalige H4-Rundscheinwerfer ist jedoch bei der Concept Ninety moderner LED-Beleuchtung gewichen. Als Würdigung der R 90 S erhielten die Karosserieteile eine Lackierung in kräftigem Seventies-Orange, das die Farbe der Ahnin zitiert und an Frontverkleidung, Tank und Heckbereich mit edel gebürstetem Aluminium kontrastiert.

Die atemberaubende Concept Ninety wurde in einem exklusiven Rahmen vorgestellt: 2013 beim Concorso d'Eleganza Villa d'Este, einem jährlich am Comer See stattfindenden Schönheitswettbewerb für die edelsten Automobile und Motorräder, präsentierte BMW Motorrad das Showbike dem versammelten Publikum. Unter gewaltigem Applaus gab sich ein außergewöhnliches Custombike die Ehre – und vermittelte zudem eine Ahnung von der noch in der Entwicklung befindlichen R nineT.

BMW Motorrad

BMW MOTORRAD PRESENTED THE SHOW BIKE AT THE 2013 CONCORSO D'ELEGANZA VILLA D'ESTE: THE EXTRAORDINARY CUSTOM BIKE INSPIRED TREMEN-DOUS APPLAUSE FROM THE CROWD.

BMW MOTORRAD PRÄSENTIERTE DAS SHOW-BIKE 2013 BEIM CONCORSO D'ELEGANZA VILLA D'ESTE: UNTER GEWALTIGEM APPLAUS GAB SICH EIN AUSSERGEWöHNLICHES CUSTOMBIKE DIE EHRE.

76
URBAN
MOTOR
BMW
brembo

URBAN
MOTOR

URBAN MOTOR
TRACK GRINDER

CUSTOMIZER	URBAN MOTOR
ESTABLISHED	2008
LOCATED	BERLIN, GERMANY
INFO	WWW.URBAN-MOTOR.DE

URBAN MOTOR TRACK GRINDER

"Urban Motor." The Berlin-based bike builders could hardly have come up with a more fitting name for their bike garage. The crew, led by Peter Dannenberg, found a truly urban location right next to the Spree river. In the small industrial area in the Rummelsburg district of Berlin, thermal power stations tower over them. As one would expect, Urban Motor creates city-conscious custom bike designs. Agile, sleek, and featuring a powerful stroke, even at low speeds. Tweaked to match traditional values while at the same time contemporary in style and design. An old twin-valve BMW is almost always used as the basis. "We have an appreciation for the classic boxer engines because they are simply practical, rock-solid, and completely suitable for daily use," says Dannenberg. After a certain point, "the classic BMW bikes were perfect for the new trend emerging throughout Europe that involves cool conversions of old bikes. And in Germany, our ideas put us at the forefront of this trend."

Although this passionate bike builder knows that modern bikes have a noticeably higher level of chassis and engine performance, he's primarily interested in vehicle designs where the manufacturers deviate from giving their bikes the typical style and avoid outfitting them with extravagant technical features and complicated electronics.

Let's rewind to the winter of 2013. The small garage (located in Berlin Mitte back then) has already received numerous visits from BMW Motorrad employees. But on this day, the Bavarian-based employees make Peter an unbelievable offer. They want him to take a pre-series specimen and use it to build the world's first R nineT custom bike. And he has no more than seven weeks to complete the task. Dannenberg doesn't have to think it over for long. He agrees, grinning from ear to ear. He runs his hand slowly over the aluminum tank and says, "We consider this a tremendous honor."

The employees at the Berlin garage had to keep quiet about all of this. After all, the public hardly knew anything about the future Heritage model series at that point. The Urban Motor crew immediately began taking measurements on the new 1200cc

URBAN MOTOR TRACK GRINDER

Urban Motor. Einen passenderen Namen für ihre Zweiradwerkstatt konnten die Berliner Schönschrauber kaum finden. Unmittelbar an der Spree gelegen, auf einem kleinen Industrieareal im Stadtteil Rummelsburg, überragt von den Türmen des Heizkraftwerks, hat sich die Crew um Peter Dannenberg einen wahrhaft urbanen Ort ausgesucht. Entsprechend stadtaffin fallen die Custombikes von Urban Motor aus. Wendig, schlank und mit kraftvollem Schlag schon bei niedrigen Drehzahlen. Auf traditionelle Werte geeicht und dabei zeitgenössisch in Stil und Ausführung. Fast immer ist eine alte Zweiventil-BMW die Basis. „Wir schätzen die klassischen Boxer, weil sie einfach praktisch sind, grundsolide und absolut alltagstauglich", so Dannenberg. Ab einem gewissen Punkt „galten die klassischen BMW für eine junge, frische Szene in ganz Europa als coole Umbaubasis. Und wir waren in Deutschland mit unseren Ideen ganz vorne dabei."

Dem leidenschaftlichen Motorradmann ist nicht entgangen, dass moderne Bikes über eine spürbar gesteigerte Fahrwerks- und Motorperformance verfügen. Ihn interessieren Neufahrzeuge aber vor allem dann, wenn es sich um Motorräder handelt, bei denen die Hersteller vom gängigen Gusto abweichen und auf eine Ausstattung mit immer üppigeren Technikfeatures und komplizierter Elektronik verzichten.

Spulen wir zurück in den Winter 2013. Schon mehrfach haben Mitarbeiter von BMW Motorrad die kleine Werkstatt – damals noch in Berlin-Mitte – besucht. Doch an jenem Tag unterbreiten die Bayern Peter ein sagenhaftes Angebot. Er werde ein Vorserienexemplar erhalten und könne daraus das erste R nineT Custombike weltweit bauen. Bis zur Fertigstellung dürfen jedoch nicht mehr als sieben Wochen Zeit vergehen. Dannenberg muss nicht lange überlegen, er willigt freudestrahlend ein. Langsam fährt er mit der Hand über den Alutank: „Wir betrachten das als eine große Ehre."

Über all das mussten die Berliner absolutes Stillschweigen bewahren, schließlich wusste die Öffentlichkeit noch kaum etwas von der zukünftigen Heritage-Modellreihe.

"WE CAME UP WITH THE CONCEPT IN ONE LONG NIGHT."

„INNERHALB EINER LANGEN NACHT STAND DAS KONZEPT."

bike. They barricaded themselves in the shop—armed with laptops, pencils, and paper. "We came up with the concept in one long night," says Dannenberg with a laugh. The decision was to reduce the bike to the most essential properties and to retain the basic sporty feel. The first step was to clean the fuel tank. A hump seat and a front fairing were created from aluminum on the in-house workbench. Stub handlebars and foot pegs that have been shifted towards the rear to accentuate the dynamic aspects. Grip tape and a skateboard wheel give the bike big-city flair. Bulky tires and a side-mounted license plate holder were added to the R nineT to give it some detail in the typical crossover style of Urban Motor. Atypical, bold, and different for a roadster. The paint job was also completely different. The Berliners used a silver base color and then sprayed over it with two lively colors from the BMW Motorrad palette: a strong blue from the '86 R 80 G/S and a piercing purple from the 1992 GS. "Clearly a polarizing decision," says the boss of Urban Motor with a smirk.

The final custom bike was given a snappy name: Track Grinder. The bright colors had dried just in time for the presentation date at the Custombike-Show in December 2013 in Bad Salzuflen. The first R nineT in a long series of Soul Fuel bikes was presented to the expert audience. Built in Berlin.

THE TRACK GRINDER IS ATYPICAL, BOLD, AND DIFFERENT FOR A ROADSTER.

FÜR EINEN ROADSTER IST DER TRACK GRINDER UNTYPISCH, FRECH, ANDERS.

Die Urban Motor Crew begann sofort damit, die fabrikneue 1200er zu vermessen und verbarrikadierte sich – bewaffnet mit Laptop, Stift und Zettel – im Laden. „Innerhalb einer langen Nacht stand das Konzept“, lacht Dannenberg. Man hatte beschlossen, das Bike aufs Wesentliche zu reduzieren und die sportliche Grundlinie beizubehalten. Zunächst wurde der Benzintank gecleant, eine Höckersitzbank und eine Frontmaske entstanden aus Aluminium auf der eigenen Werkbank. Stummellenker und zurückverlegte Fußrasten betonen die dynamische Seite. Griptape und Skateboardrolle sorgen für Großstadtflair. Um den typischen Crossover-Stil von Urban Motor herauszuarbeiten, erhielt die R nineT grobstollige Reifen und einen seitlichen Kennzeichenhalter. Für einen Roadster untypisch, frech, anders. Völlig anders wurde auch die Lackierung: Auf eine silberne Grundfarbe sprayten die Hauptstädter zwei mutige Farbtöne aus der BMW Motorrad Palette: ein kräftiges Blau von der ’86er R 80 G/S und ein schrilles Violett von der GS aus dem Jahr 1992. „Klar, das polarisiert“, grinst der Urban-Chef.

Das fertige Custombike erhielt den markigen Namen Track Grinder, frei übersetzt: Strecken-Schleifer. Pünktlich zum Präsentationstermin auf der Custombike-Show im im Dezember 2013 in Bad Salzuflen war die grelle Farbe gerade noch trocken geworden. Die erste R nineT in einer langen Reihe von Soul Fuel Bikes stellte sich dem fachkundigen Publikum. Gebaut in Berlin.

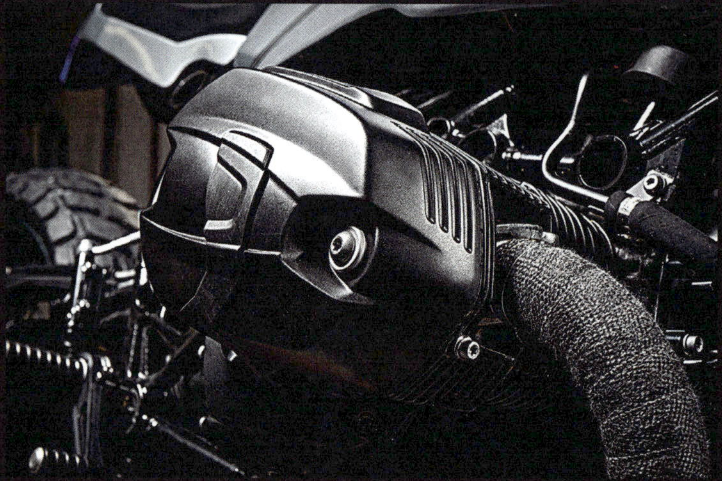

STUB HANDLEBARS AND FOOT PEGS THAT HAVE BEEN SHIFTED TOWARDS THE REAR TO ACCENTUATE THE DYNAMIC ASPECTS. GRIP TAPE AND A SKATEBOARD WHEEL GIVE THE BIKE BIG-CITY FLAIR.

STUMMELLENKER UND ZURÜCKVERLEGTE FUSSRASTEN BETONEN DIE DYNAMISCHE SEITE. GRIPTAPE UND SKATEBOARDROLLE SORGEN FÜR GROSSSTADTFLAIR.

EL SOLITARIO
IMPOSTOR
RAGE IS BOLD
WITH GOLD?
FIND
THEN AWAY FROM THIS

W.T.F.

EL SOLITARIO MOTOR CO.
IMPOSTOR

CUSTOMIZER	EL SOLITARIO MOTOR CO.
ESTABLISHED	2010
LOCATED	VIGO, SPAIN
INFO	WWW.ELSOLITARIOMC.COM

EL SOLITARIO MOTOR CO.
IMPOSTOR

El Solitario Motor Co.—this is not your ordinary motorcycle workshop. In the world of customizing, these Galicians are a phenomenon. At their workshop in Vigo, Spain, the team led by David Borras and Valeria Libano develops and builds what are perhaps the most uncompromising one-of-a-kind specimens on the worldwide scene of custom bikes. Time after time the visionary—and sometimes controversial—creations trigger lively discussions about how meaningful or absurd radical motorcycle modifications are. For example, ardent fans who admire El Solitario for not caring about the mainstream and the opinions of others argue with conservative motorcyclists. The latter aren't pleased with the artistic insanity designed into the motorcycles. "We do not follow the trends, we dictate them," says David in response to his critics. How right he is. Anyone who takes a closer look at the creations of him and his team comes to understand that El Solitario is the "real deal," a team of passionate individualists, the wild artists of the custom scene. And at the same time—extraordinarily fun.

Since 2010 the two founders have been occupied with the redesign of motorcycles. Under the force of their own lifestyle, which revolves around skateboarding, heavy metal, and fast bikes, they quickly came to develop their own signature style. This is because, for El Solitario, riding motorcycles is not just the embodiment of speed, but also a spiritual domain that inspires people to creativity and emotional power. The bikes that leave the Galicians' garage are the counter concept to stock motorcycles, mass production, and the cookie-cutter look. Therefore every El Solitario bike remains one-of-a-kind. In explaining the idea behind the brand, the full-bearded boss says, "We are neither a fashion brand nor a motorcycle company. El Solitario is just the umbrella underneath which we develop our creative ethos."

Late in 2013 BMW Motorrad became aware of the radical bike projects of El Solitario. They received the order to design a standalone custom bike based on the new R nineT. The one of a kind order was to be completed by February of 2014, in time to be presented at the fifth One Motorcycle Show in Oregon (USA). Borras and his team then spent

EL SOLITARIO MOTOR CO.
IMPOSTOR

El Solitario Motor Co., das ist keine der üblichen Motorrad-Werkstätten. In der Welt des Customizings sind die Galicier ein Phänomen. Das Team um David Borras und Valeria Libano entwickelt und fertigt in seiner Werkstatt im spanischen Vigo die vielleicht kompromisslosesten Unikate der weltweiten Custombike-Szene. Immer wieder regen die visionären, teils umstrittenen Kreationen zu lebhaften Diskussionen über den Sinn und Unsinn von radikalen Motorradumbauten an. So streiten sich glühende Fans, die El Solitario dafür bewundern, dass sie sich nicht um den Mainstream und die Meinung anderer kümmern, mit konservativen Motorradfahrern. Denen missfällt der in die Motorräder hineinkonstruierte künstlerische Wahnsinn. „Wir laufen den Trends nicht hinterher, wir diktieren sie", antwortet David seinen Kritikern. Wie recht er damit hat. Denn wer sich die Kreationen von ihm und seinem Team genauer anschaut, der begreift ziemlich schnell: El Solitario sind der „Real Deal", leidenschaftliche Individualisten, die wilden Künstler der Custom-Szene. Und dabei außergewöhnlich unterhaltsam.

Seit 2010 befassen sich die beiden Gründer mit der Neugestaltung von Motorrädern. Unter dem Einfluss ihrer Begeisterung für Skateboarding, Metal-Sound und schnelle Bikes entwickelten sie einen unverkennbaren Stil. Denn für El Solitario ist Motorradfahren nicht nur der Inbegriff von Speed, sondern auch ein spirituelles Feld, das zu Kreativität und emotionaler Kraft inspiriert. Die Bikes, die die Garage der Galicier verlassen, sind der Gegenentwurf zu Serienmotorrädern, zu Massenproduktion und Einheitslook. Daher bleibt jedes El Solitario Bike ein Unikat. „Wir sind weder ein Fashion Brand noch eine Motorcycle Company", beschreibt der vollbärtige Chef die Idee hinter der Marke, „El Solitario ist nur der Regenschirm, unter dem wir unser kreatives Ethos entwickeln."

Ende 2013 wurde BMW Motorrad auf die radikalen Bike-Projekte von El Solitario aufmerksam. Sie erhielten den Auftrag, ein eigenständiges Custombike auf Basis der neuen R nineT zu gestalten. Bis Februar 2014, zur fünften The One Motorcycle Show in

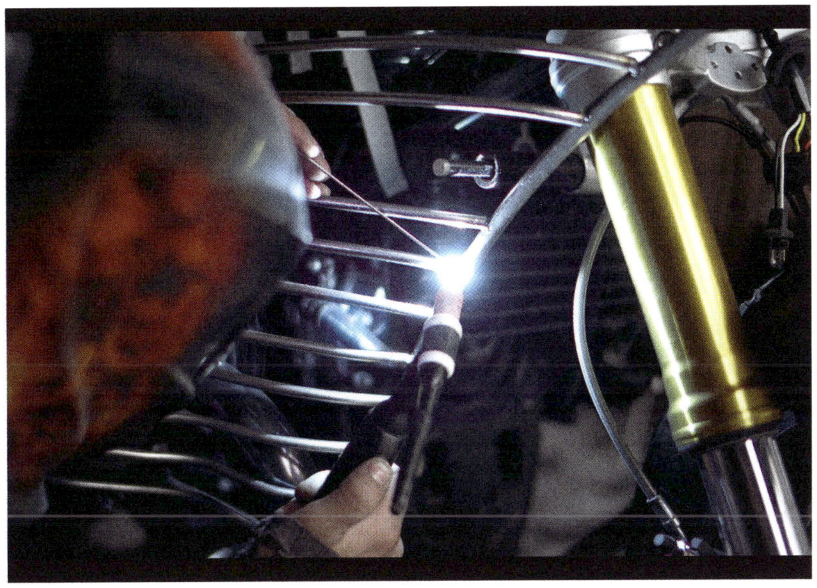

“WE DO NOT FOLLOW THE TRENDS, WE DICTATE THEM.”

„WIR LAUFEN DEN TRENDS NICHT HINTERHER, WIR DIKTIEREN SIE.“

around 80 days and more than 700 hours in the workshop to take the roadster and create the Impostor—a full-on stand-alone. “The Impostor is Attila's horse. Strong, excessive, raw, and merciless. And so the R nineT also becomes a wicked machine, which nevertheless does everything to protect its rider.” David reports that the design process was also significantly influenced by bōsōzoku gangs, a Japanese motorcycle subculture, as well as by endurance racers from the 1970s.

“The R nineT is a fantastic motorcycle and already looks perfect in its original stance. However, it was the newest platform on which we had ever worked,” recalls the good-humored Spaniard. “We had to adapt our creative process to it.” Therefore, with the exception of the wheels, the mechanics touched neither the suspension nor the engine, transmission or shaft drive. They did not drill any additional holes into the functional components, and they left the wiring harness untouched. Instead, they concentrated on the packaging of the BMW. “The motorcycle remained a totally original R nineT, which any BMW-authorized mechanic can service with their eyes closed,” David says to reassure skeptics, who, upon seeing the extreme custom bike, have misgivings about its suitability for daily use.

“While all the components for a bōsōzoku chopper racer were being mixed, the idea came about to emulate the bodywork silhouette in the form of a skeleton,” says David with a grin. So he and his team sawed, shaped, and welded many meters of tubular stainless steel into a sculpture that encloses the entire motorcycle, even the two cylinders of the opposed-twin engine—reminiscent of perforated racing cover paneling with racing seat. They densely covered the gas tank, painted only with primer, with engravings. A 21-inch front wheel replaces the standard 17-inch one, and a full 16-inch wheel is used for the rear. The adjustable fork of BMW's supersport motorcycle S 1000 RR provides the Impostor with optimized riding characteristics. Four compact LED headlights are concealed behind the panel grating. Couched on the right next to the front wheel there is also a single Marchal fog light with yellow glass.

With a look of irony on his face David Borras says, “We want to make people feel a shock—an impact—when they see this motorcycle. Whether it is pleasing to the eye is less important.”

Oregon, USA, sollte das Einzelstück fertiggestellt sein und dort präsentiert werden. Rund 80 Tage und mehr als 700 Stunden verbrachten Borras und sein Team von nun an in der Werkstatt, um aus dem Roadster die völlig eigenständige Impostor entstehen zu lassen. „Die Impostor ist wie Attilas Pferd. Stark, exzessiv, rau und gnadenlos. So soll auch die R nineT eine böse Maschine werden, die jedoch alles dafür tut, ihren Fahrer zu beschützen“, so David. Auch Bōsōzoku-Gangs, eine japanische Motorradsubkultur, sowie Endurance-Racer der 1970er-Jahre hätten den Gestaltungsprozess maßgeblich beeinflusst.

„Die R nineT ist ein fantastisches Motorrad und sieht schon im Original perfekt aus. Allerdings war sie die neueste Plattform, an der wir je gearbeitet haben“, erinnert sich der stets gut gelaunte Spanier. „Wir mussten unseren kreativen Prozess daran anpassen.“ Daher rührten die Mechaniker mit Ausnahme der Räder weder das Fahrwerk noch Motor, Getriebe oder Kardanantrieb an. Sie bohrten nicht ein zusätzliches Loch in die funktionalen Komponenten und ließen auch den Kabelbaum unangetastet. Stattdessen konzentrierten sie sich auf die Verpackung der BMW. „Das Motorrad ist eine vollkommen originale R nineT geblieben, die von jedem BMW Vertragspartner mit geschlossenen Augen gewartet werden kann“, beruhigt David die Skeptiker, die beim Anblick des extremen Custombikes an dessen Alltagstauglichkeit zweifeln.

„Beim Mixen aller Komponenten zu einem Bōsōzoku-Chopper-Racer entstand die Idee, die Silhouette des Bodyworks in Form eines Skeletts nachzubilden“, grinst David. Also sägten, formten und schweißten er und seine Mannschaft viele Meter Edelstahlrohr zu einer Skulptur, die das gesamte Motorrad, ja selbst die beiden Zylinder des Boxermotors umschließt und die an eine perforierte Rennverkleidung samt Höckersitzbank erinnert. Den lediglich grundierten Tank übersäten sie mit Gravuren. Ein 21-Zoll-Vorderrad ersetzt den serienmäßigen Siebzehnzöller, hinten kommt ein fülliges 16-Zoll-Rad zum Einsatz. Verbesserte Fahreigenschaften bietet eine einstellbare Gabel des BMW Supersportlers S 1000 RR, vier kompakte LED-Scheinwerfer verstecken sich hinter dem Verkleidungsgitter. Rechts neben dem Vorderrad kauert zudem ein einzelner Marchal-Nebelscheinwerfer mit gelbem Glas.

Mit ironischem Gesichtsausdruck sagt David Borras: „Mit diesem Motorrad wollen wir einen Schock beim Betrachter provozieren, einen Impact. Das heißt aber nicht unbedingt, dass wir ihm einen Augenschmeichler präsentieren wollen.“

„WHILE ALL THE COMPONENTS FOR A BŌSŌZOKU CHOPPER RACER WERE BEING MIXED, THE IDEA CAME ABOUT TO EMULATE THE BODYWORK SILHOUETTE IN THE FORM OF A SKELETON."

„BEIM MIXEN ALLER KOMPONENTEN ZU EINEM BŌSŌZOKU-CHOPPER-RACER ENTSTAND DIE IDEE, DIE SILHOUETTE DES BODYWORKS IN FORM EINES SKELETTS NACHZUBILDEN."

“THE IMPOSTOR IS ATTILA’S HORSE. STRONG, EXCESSIVE, RAW, AND MERCILESS.”

„DIE IMPOSTOR IST WIE ATTILAS PFERD. STARK, EXZESSIV, RAU UND GNADENLOS.“

BLITZ MOTORCYCLES
9 TRACKER

CUSTOMIZER	BLITZ MOTORCYCLES
ESTABLISHED	2010
LOCATED	PARIS, FRANCE
INFO	WWW.BLITZ-MOTORCYCLES.COM

LAID-BACK, MONOCHROMATIC, AND EQUIPPED ONLY WITH THE ESSENTIAL MOUNTED PARTS

LÄSSIG, MONOCHROM UND NUR MIT DEN NöTIGSTEN ANBAUTEILEN BESTÜCKT

BLITZ MOTORCYCLES
9 TRACKER

The French love taking classic BMW bikes and turning them into custom creations. In addition to a few German bike builders, they were the ones who worked with fervor and passion to firmly establish the twin-valve boxer of the /5 through /7 series on the customizing scene. That's not all: Ever since French tinkerers demonstrated how to transform tame and classic touring bikes into cool, minimalistic, and unique works of art, BMW motorcycles have evolved into a favorite within the new-wave custom subculture spread across Europe.

Fred Jourden and Hugo Jezegabel founded Blitz Motorcycles in the center of Paris in 2010, and they, too, strongly favored the robust twin-valve BMW engines. In the corner of a basement garage, the two of them gave life to their distinct and unmistakable Blitz style: laid-back, monochromatic, and equipped only with the essential mounted parts.

At the end of 2013, the Frenchmen were pleasantly surprised by a request from BMW Motorrad asking them to devise their own modification for a pilot series R nineT. Before then, these bike builders had only converted classic BMW bikes. Working with a new vehicle with an anti-lock braking system and fuel injection feature required them to gain some familiarity first. Fortunately, the BMW Motorrad engineers intentionally gave the R nineT a tinkerer-friendly design. As a result, converting the new model ended up taking less effort than expected. Fred and Hugo could devote most of their time—and enthusiasm—to focusing on the aesthetic modifications. The goal was to turn the standard roadster into a tracker, a reduced sports bike in the style of an American track racer. "We modeled our work after the classic flat trackers from the 1970s," said Fred. "The idea behind this was not to make the motorcycle look like an R nineT, but to create a look that would amaze people."

BLITZ MOTORCYCLES
9 TRACKER

Franzosen lieben es, klassische BMW Motorräder in individuelle Einzelstücke zu verwandeln. Neben einigen deutschen Bike-Buildern waren sie es, die intensiv und passioniert dazu beigetragen haben, Zweiventil-Boxer der „Strich-Fünf"- bis „Strich-Sieben"-Baureihe fest in der Customizing-Szene zu etablieren. Mehr noch: Seit französische Schrauber kurz nach der Jahrtausendwende gezeigt haben, wie man aus kreuzbraven Tourern minimalistische und coole Unikate zaubern kann, entwickelten sich die bayerischen Motorräder zu den Lieblingen der New-Custom-Subkultur in ganz Europa.

Fred Jourden und Hugo Jezegabel gründeten 2010 Blitz Motorcycles im Zentrum von Paris, und auch sie stürzten sich umgehend auf die robusten Zweiventiler von BMW. In der Ecke einer Tiefgarage realisierten die beiden ihr ganz spezielles und unverwechselbares Blitz-Styling: lässig, monochrom und nur mit den nötigsten Anbauteilen bestückt.

Ende 2013 überraschte die Anfrage von BMW Motorrad, doch bitte eine Vorserien-R nineT nach eigenen Vorstellungen zu modifizieren, die Franzosen. Bis dahin hatten sie ausschließlich klassische BMW Motorräder umgebaut; an ein Neufahrzeug mit ABS und Benzineinspritzung mussten sie sich erst einmal herantasten. Glücklicherweise hatten die Ingenieure von BMW Motorrad die R nineT gezielt schrauberfreundlich gestaltet, sodass der Arbeitsaufwand beim Umbau der Neuen weniger aufwendig ausfiel als erwartet. Fred und Hugo konnten sich voller Enthusiasmus den optischen Modifikationen widmen. Denn aus dem serienmäßigen Roadster sollte ein Tracker werden, ein reduziertes Sportmotorrad im Stil der amerikanischen Bahnrenner. „Als Vorbild dienten uns die klassischen Flat-Tracker aus den 1970er-Jahren", so Fred. „Die Idee dahinter war, das Motorrad nicht wie eine R nineT aussehen zu lassen, sondern wie etwas, das die Menschen erstaunt."

"WE MODELED OUR WORK AFTER THE CLASSIC FLAT TRACKERS FROM THE 1970S"

„ALS VORBILD DIENTEN UNS DIE KLASSISCHEN FLAT-TRACKER AUS DEN 1970ER-JAHREN"

9T

When creating the fuel tank—a significant design feature for the tracker—the pair of Frenchmen forged entirely new paths. They consulted a specialist in the area of rapid prototyping and, after a few drafts, had the tank 3D-printed using polyamide. The sports tank was created layer-by-layer and then just had to be sealed from the inside by the boys at Blitz.

Another goal was to use K&N air filters to filter the intake air instead of the bulky air box. Installing a 2-in-1 race exhaust system made it necessary to re-tune the engine control—a process that required special BMW diagnostics equipment. The bike builders made the rear frame shorter to allow the use of a racing seat with sharper aesthetics. In addition, they decided to use 19-inch rims, adapted to the original R nineT hubs. They put special flat track tires on the wheels. Straight, wide handlebars without bar switches was used to help achieve the "pure" visual that was desired.

Almost all parts were given a jet black coat of paint or plastic covering. Even the fork bridges, footpegs, handlebars, and engine components were given a dark powder coating, giving the 9 Tracker its no-frills, understated, elegant, and exceptionally laid-back look. The R nineT conversion does more than mark another successful and stylish Blitz bike for Fred and Hugo. It also serves as definitive proof of the passion these Frenchmen feel for the boxer motorcycles made by BMW.

Bei der Herstellung eines Benzintanks als wesentliches Gestaltungsmerkmal ihres Trackers gingen die beiden Franzosen völlig neue Wege. Sie wandten sich an einen Spezialisten auf dem Gebiet des Rapid Prototyping und ließen den Behälter nach eigenen Entwürfen im 3-D-Druck aus Polyamid anfertigen. Der Schicht für Schicht entstandene Sporttank musste anschließend von den Blitz-Jungs nur noch von innen versiegelt werden.

Statt der voluminösen Airbox sollten zudem K&N-Luftfilter die Ansaugluft filtern. Die Montage einer 2-in-1-Rennauspuffanlage machte eine Neuabstimmung der Motorsteuerung nötig, wozu es spezieller Diagnostikausrüstung von BMW bedurfte. Um einen knackigen Rennsitz verwenden zu können, kürzten die Schrauber den Heckrahmen. Außerdem entschieden sie sich für die Verwendung von 19-Zoll-Felgen, angepasst an die originalen R nineT-Radnaben. Auf die Räder zogen sie spezielle Flat-Track-Bereifung. Ein gerader, breiter Lenker, bei dem auf Lenkerschalter verzichtet wurde, unterstützt die gewünschte cleane Optik.

Fast alle Teile wurden mit einem tiefschwarzen Farb- oder Kunststoffüberzug versehen. Auch Gabelbrücken, Fußrasten, Lenkerhalter und Motorkomponenten erhielten eine dunkle Pulverbeschichtung, wodurch die 9 Tracker schlicht, unaufdringlich elegant und sehr lässig daherkommt. Fred und Hugo ist mit dem R nineT-Umbau nicht nur ein weiteres, ausgefallenes Blitz-Bike gelungen, sondern gleichzeitig ein eindrucksvoller Beleg für die Liebe der Franzosen zu den Boxer-Motorrädern aus dem Hause BMW.

Roland Sands Design

ROLAND SANDS DESIGN
R NINE T CLASSIC

CUSTOMIZER	ROLAND SANDS DESIGN
ESTABLISHED	2005
LOCATED	LOS ALAMITOS, CA, USA
INFO	WWW.ROLANDSANDS.COM

brembo
DUNLOP

"I'LL HELP EXPLAIN TO AMERICANS WHAT THE R NINE T IS ALL ABOUT."
„ICH WERDE MITHELFEN, DEN AMERIKANERN ZU ERKLÄREN, FÜR WAS DIE R NINE T STEHT."

ROLAND SANDS DESIGN R NINE T CLASSIC

Roland Sands, the fast riding motorcyclist and talented designer from California, has obviously left a lasting impression with those-in-charge at BMW Motorrad. After he had lent his support to the design team during the development of the sensational Concept Ninety, he was soon after asked if he would like to design and build his own custom bike on the basis of a pre-production R nineT. Sands recalls: "I saw the motorcycle and ideas started flowing through my head immediately. I became even more excited after I rode the motorcycle for the first time. The unfiltered dynamics and the full torque completely floored me. The R nineT is a great machine and marks BMW's return to a more stylish, soul driven machine."

For the head of Roland Sands Design (RSD), this task was not only about accolades—he also used the project simultaneously as a platform to develop his projected series of accessories for the R nineT. With his eye on a U.S. market eager to customize, Sands was thoroughly convinced that the success of BMW's Heritage series would also depend on the scope of the program for accessories. "American customers love to modify their machines. The easier manufacturers make it for their customers the more these machines are in demand," observes Sands. Therefore, it was also important to the bike builder to develop parts that can be installed with minimum effort: "I wanted to look at the motorcycle from the customer's perspective and at what can be modified without professional tools. I was interested in what the owner can do with the R nineT without having to delve too deeply into the subject matter and without impeding the well-rounded functionality of machine."

And so the RSD team designed an entire series of individualized and high-quality accessory parts for the new BMW, including CNC-machined valve and engine covers, a customized headlight, a sport exhaust system, and a milled fuel tank cover. Sands even replaced inconspicuous details with self-made parts, such as the rear torque arm

ROLAND SANDS DESIGN R NINE T CLASSIC

Roland Sands, der schnelle Motorradfahrer und begabte Designer aus Kalifornien, hat offensichtlich einen nachhaltigen Eindruck bei den Verantwortlichen von BMW Motorrad hinterlassen. Denn nachdem er dem Designteam bei der Entwicklung der sensationellen Concept Ninety zur Seite gestanden hatte, erhielt er schon bald darauf die Anfrage, ob er nicht eigenhändig ein Custombike auf Basis einer Vorserien-R nineT entwerfen und bauen wolle. Sands erinnert sich: „Ich habe das Motorrad gesehen und sofort strömten die Ideen nur so durch mein Hirn. Noch aufgeregter wurde ich, als ich das Motorrad zum ersten Mal fahren konnte. Die ungefilterte Dynamik und das satte Drehmoment begeisterten mich restlos. Mit der R nineT kehrt BMW zurück zu Motorrädern mit ausgeprägtem Stil und viel Seele."

Für den Chef von Roland Sands Design (RSD) bedeutete dieser Auftrag nicht nur einen Ritterschlag, er nutzte das Projekt gleichzeitig als Entwicklungsplattform für seine geplante Zubehörserie für die R nineT. Den umbaufreudigen US-Markt im Blick, war Sands fest davon überzeugt, dass der Erfolg der Heritage-Serie von BMW auch vom Umfang des Zubehörprogramms abhängig sein werde. „Amerikanische Kunden lieben es, ihre Maschinen zu modifizieren. Je einfacher der Hersteller es seinen Kunden macht, umso mehr wird diese Maschine nachgefragt", erläutert Sands seine Beobachtungen. Daher war es dem Bike-Builder auch wichtig, Teile zu entwickeln, die ohne großen Aufwand montiert werden können: „Ich wollte aus der Kundenperspektive auf das Motorrad schauen und darauf, was man ohne Profiwerkzeug alles verändern kann. Mich interessierte, was der Besitzer mit seiner R nineT anstellen kann, ohne tief in die Materie eintauchen zu müssen und ohne die ausgewogene Funktionalität der Maschine zu beeinträchtigen."

Also gestaltete das RSD-Team eine ganze Reihe individueller und qualitativ hochwertiger Zubehörteile für die neue BMW, darunter CNC-gefräste Ventil- und Stirndeckel,

and the ends of the handlebars. It strikes you right away that all of the RSD accessory parts do not look like some outlandish custom parts that were made in a backyard workshop, but more like exceptional, first-class finished series production parts. Additionally, the American ensured a well-rounded overall concept with a targeted color scheme. For the fuel tank paint, he chose a technoid, black/silver custom paint job; the upside-down fork sliders and the shift and brake levers got a black coat of paint.

Sands believes that R nineT engineering is absolutely sophisticated, reliable, and high-performance: "I didn't see any reason to change anything with the motor, brakes, or chassis," says the former racer, waving such notions aside. "The café racer and urban style bikes are especially popular in Europe right now." Sands points to a polished chrome long fork chopper: "But here in the U.S. the market is still dominated by big V-twin engines. I'll help explain to Americans what the R nineT is all about."

einen individuellen Scheinwerfer, eine Sportauspuffanlage und den ebenfalls gefrästen Tankdeckel. Selbst unscheinbare Details wie die hintere Drehmomentstütze oder Lenkerenden ersetzte Sands durch selbst gefertigte Teile. Auffällig ist, dass sämtliche RSD-Zubehörteile nicht etwa wie abgedrehte Custom-Parts aus einer Hinterhofwerkstatt wirken, sondern eher wie außergewöhnlich edel verarbeitete Serienteile. Zusätzlich sorgte der Amerikaner mit einer gezielten Farbgestaltung für ein ausgewogenes Gesamtkonzept. Bei der Tanklackierung entschied er sich für ein technoides, schwarz-silbernes Custom-Painting, die Tauchrohre der Upside-down-Gabel sowie Schalt- und Bremshebel erhielten einen schwarzen Lacküberzug.

Die Technik der R nineT hält Sands für absolut ausgereift, zuverlässig und leistungsstark: „Ich sah keinen Grund, irgendetwas an Motor, Bremsen oder Fahrwerk zu verändern", winkt der ehemalige Rennfahrer ab. „Vor allem in Europa sind der Café-Racer- und der Urban-Style momentan sehr populär". Sands zeigt auf einen chromglänzenden Langgabel-Chopper: „Aber bei uns in den USA wird der Markt noch immer von großen V-Zweizylindern beherrscht. Ich werde mithelfen, den Amerikanern zu erklären, für was die R nineT steht."

“I LOOK AT THE MOTORCYCLE FROM THE CUSTOMER’S PERSPECTIVE.”

„ICH SCHAUE AUS DER KUNDENPER-SPEKTIVE AUF DAS MOTORRAD.“

RSD ACCESSORY PARTS LOOK LIKE EXCEPTIONAL, FIRST-CLASS FINISHED SERIES PRODUCTION PARTS.

RSD-ZUBEHöRTEILE WIRKEN WIE AUSSERGEWöHNLICH EDEL VERARBEITETE SERIENTEILE.

BMW Motorrad

UNIQUE CUSTOM CYCLES
STOCKHOLM SYNDROME

CUSTOMIZER	**UNIQUE CUSTOM CYCLES**
ESTABLISHED	**1995**
LOCATED	**BRO, SWEDEN**
INFO	**WWW.UCCYCLES.COM**

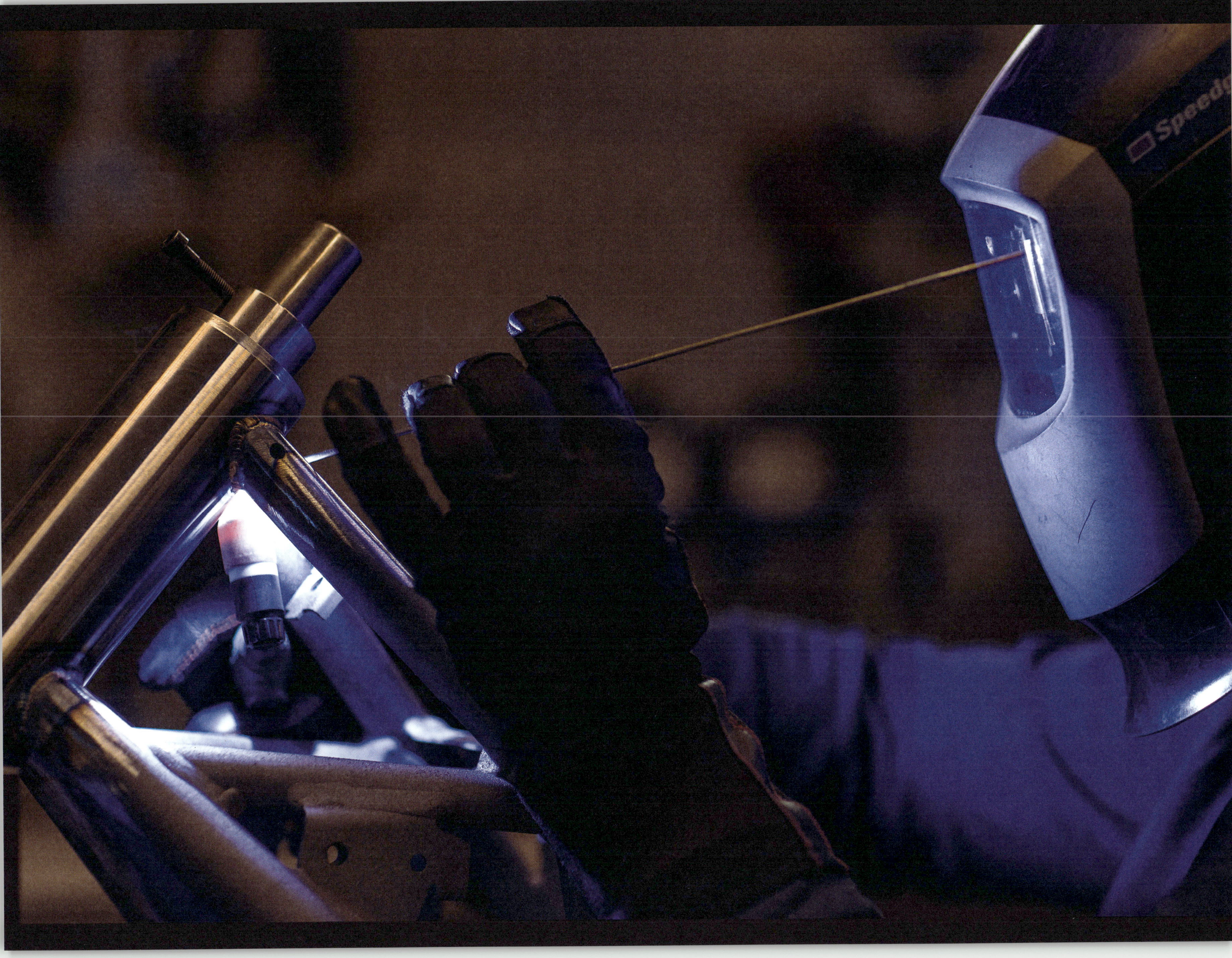

ALL KINDS OF HIGH-END SWEDISH TECHNOLOGY

JEDE MENGE SCHWEDISCHER HIGHEND-TECHNIK

UNIQUE CUSTOM CYCLES STOCKHOLM SYNDROME

Since the late 1970s, Ronna Norén and Gordon Roth have become an integral part of Scandinavian biker culture. Their first chopper projects were featured in custom chopper magazines as early as 1981. In 1995, they founded the custom bike building company Unique Custom Cycles (UCC). It's hardly a surprise that UCC is usually associated with long-fork choppers in the typical "neat" Swedish style. The brand also boasts some of the fastest European drag bikes: Street bikes, pro-stocks, supercharged top-fuelers, and powerful super twin monsters. Since 2014, the Scandinavian duo has even been redesigning BMW motorcycles. These bike builders from Bro (an urban area located 45 kilometers northwest of Stockholm) have made a habit of creating boxer-based customizations. It all started when BMW Motorrad sent them a request asking the chopper specialists if they wanted to redesign an R nineT and turn it into a one-off special entirely of their own making.

The masterminds behind UCC knew early on that they didn't want to turn the R nineT into a chopper or anything similar, but rather a traditional, sleek café racer. "The custom roadster scene is growing continually and bringing new, fresh blood into the motorcycle community," says a delighted Ronna. "This is a good thing for all of us. It takes us back to the 1970s and '80s, when being interested in motorcycles was all about having fun and about modifying bikes to fit your own taste."

This mentality led to the UCC team developing a classic sports line. However, they also wanted to outfit the bike with all kinds of high-end Swedish technology. To reach this goal, the Swedes brought some of the country's best accessory manufacturers on board. Stockholm Syndrome, as the project came to be known, called for a telescopic fork with fork bridges elongated by three degrees from Tolle Engineering. In addition, a special strut and a steering damper in typical gold plating were developed by Öhlins, an internationally renowned shock absorber specialist. The entire front brake system

UNIQUE CUSTOM CYCLES STOCKHOLM SYNDROME

Seit Ende der 1970er-Jahre sind Ronna Norén und Gordon Roth eng mit der skandinavischen Biker-Kultur verwachsen. Ihre ersten Chopper-Kreationen schmückten bereits 1981 die Custom-Magazine. 1995 gründeten sie die Custom-Manufaktur Unique Custom Cycles (UCC). So verwundert es kaum, dass mit UCC normalerweise Langgabel-Chopper im typischen, sauberen Schweden-Stil verbunden werden. Außerdem steht die Marke für einige der schnellsten europäischen Dragbikes: Streetbikes, Pro-Stocks, aufgeladene Top-Fueler und gewaltige Super-Twin-Monster. Doch seit 2014 befassen sich die Skandinavier aus Bro, 45 Kilometer nordwestlich von Stockholm gelegen, auch mit der Umgestaltung von BMW Motorrädern. Startschuss dafür war die Anfrage von BMW Motorrad, ob die Chopper-Spezialisten eine R nineT in ein Einzelstück verwandeln wollten.

Schnell stand für die Männer hinter UCC fest, dass aus der R nineT nicht etwa ein Chopper werden sollte, sondern ein traditioneller, schlanker Cafe Racer. „Die Custom-Roadster-Szene wächst kontinuierlich und bringt neues und junges Blut in die Motorrad-Community", freut sich Ronna. „Das ist gut für uns alle. Es erinnert uns an die 1970er- und 80er-Jahre, als es beim Motorradfahren einfach nur um Spaß ging und darum, ein Motorrad nach dem eigenen Geschmack zu verändern."

Das UCC-Team entwarf daher eine klassisch-sportliche Linie, wollte das Bike aber mit jeder Menge schwedischer Highend-Technik bestücken. Um dieses Ziel zu erreichen, nahm man einige der besten Zubehörhersteller des Landes mit ins Boot. Das Stockholm Syndrome getaufte Projekt sollte eine Telegabel mit um drei Grad gereckten Gabelbrücken von Tolle Engineering erhalten. Zudem entwickelte der international anerkannte Stoßdämpferspezialist Öhlins ein spezielles Federbein und einen Lenkungsdämpfer in typischer Goldoberfläche für die 1200er BMW. Die komplette vordere Bremsanlage samt Sechskolbenzangen, schwimmend gelagerter 320-mm-Scheiben mit integrierten

BMW
Unique Custom Cycles
ME 880

THE MASTERMINDS BEHIND UCC KNEW EARLY ON THAT THEY DIDN'T WANT TO TURN THE R NINE T INTO A CHOPPER, BUT RATHER A TRADITIONAL, SLEEK CAFÉ RACER.

FÜR DIE MÄNNER HINTER UCC STAND SCHNELL FEST, DASS AUS DER R NINE T KEIN CHOPPER WERDEN SOLLTE, SONDERN EIN TRADITIONELLER, SCHLANKER CAFE RACER.

along with the six-piston caliper, the 320 mm discs with floating bearings and built-in ABS sensors as well as the fully adjustable braking and coupling cylinder were all supplied by ISR Brakes.

Because the customizers had a “café racer” look in mind, they opted to use spoked wheels in classic dimensions: 19 inches in the front and 18 inches in the rear. They separated the steering head from the frame and offset it by a few degrees so as not to negatively affect the bike’s naturally agile riding characteristics. In combination with the elongated Tolle fork, the scrupulous Swedes made sure that superb handling and reliable directional stability were maintained.

In their own workshop, Ronna and Gordon also created a shorter rear frame, a one-person seat and the bent piping. In addition, they installed an oil cooler from their accessory product range. They took special care when designing the fuel tank. Although it is based on the original fuel tank, it has a more dynamic effect thanks to a “flatter” silhouette. This sleeker tank design required repositioning the air box and the electrical system, too. Ronna says, “Creating the fuel tank wasn’t difficult. It was a normal job for us. We generally don’t have any trouble designing and building components. The only real problem we had during the Stockholm Syndrome project was the lack of time.” This is because UCC had exactly five weeks to turn the R nineT into a café racer. Thirty-five days of near-constant work and next to no sleep for Ronna and Gordon. The project was urgent because it had to be ready in time for the annual Custom Bike Show in Norrtälje, Sweden, one of the country’s most important bike shows. Despite the limited time frame, the unmatched perfection of Stockholm Syndrome earned it second place among the many entrants in the “Custom Class” and got the UCC crew thinking about the possibility of more BMW custom bikes.

ABS-Sensoren und vollständig justierbarer Brems- und Kupplungszylinder lieferte ISR Brakes.

Wegen der geplanten Cafe-Racer-Optik entschieden sich die Customizer für die Verwendung von Speichenrädern in klassischen Dimensionen – vorne 19 Zoll und hinten 18 Zoll. Um das von Haus aus agile Fahrverhalten nicht zu verwässern, trennten sie den Lenkkopf vom Rahmen und versetzten ihn um wenige Winkelgrade. In Kombination mit der gereckten Tolle-Gabel stellten die peniblen Schweden sicher, dass superbes Handling und stabiler Geradeauslauf beibehalten werden.

In der eigenen Werkstatt fertigten Ronna und Gordon einen kürzeren Heckrahmen, eine Einmannsitzbank und die Krümmerrohre, außerdem montierten sie einen Ölkühler aus dem eigenen Zubehörprogramm. Besonderes Augenmerk legten sie auf den Benzintank, der zwar auf dem originalen Spritbehälter basiert, durch seine flachere Silhouette aber dynamischer wirkt. Wegen der schlankeren Tankform mussten Airbox und Elektrik neu positioniert werden. Dazu Ronna: „Die Fertigung des Benzintanks war nicht schwierig, das ist für uns ein normaler Job. Generell fällt es uns nicht schwer, Komponenten zu entwickeln und zu bauen. Wenn wir ein Problem beim Bau der ‚Stockholm Syndrome' hatten, dann war es die mangelnde Zeit." Denn UCC hatte gerade einmal fünf Wochen, um die R nineT in einen Cafe Racer zu verwandeln. 35 Tage, an denen Ronna und Gordon beinahe rund um die Uhr gearbeitet und äußerst wenig geschlafen haben. Der Grund für die Eile war die alljährlich stattfindende Custom Bike Show in Norrtälje, eine der wichtigsten Bikeshows des Landes. Mit ihrer – trotz der kurzen Bauzeit – unnachahmlichen Perfektion belegte Stockholm Syndrome den zweiten Platz in der dicht besetzten „Custom Class" – und machte die UCC-Crew ganz nebenbei neugierig auf weitere BMW Customs.

FOUR OF THE MOST TALENTED JAPANESE CUSTOMIZERS. TO EACH THEIR OWN BIKE. THE "PROJECT JAPAN."

VIER DER BEGABTESTEN JAPANISCHEN CUSTOMIZER. JEDER EIN EIGENES BIKE. DAS „PROJECT JAPAN“.

brembo

CHERRY'S COMPANY
HIGHWAY FIGHTER

CUSTOMIZER	**CHERRY'S COMPANY**
ESTABLISHED	**2000**
LOCATED	**TOKYO, JAPAN**
INFO	**WWW.CHERRYSCOMPANY.COM**

CHERRY'S COMPANY
HIGHWAY FIGHTER

February 2014. Four Japanese bike builders are sitting on a sofa and a few chairs across from one another, flanked by a couple of BMW Motorrad employees. The four are waiting to see and get a feel for the new BMW R nineT for the first time. Shiro Nakajima from 46 Works, Hidemo boss Hideya Togashi, the Brat Style man Go Takamine and Kaichiroh Kurosu from Cherry's Company have come together at the invitation of the German motorcycle company to discuss the design concept, and to redesign the Boxer bike according to their own conceptions. Four of the most talented Japanese customizers. To each their own bike. The "Project Japan."

When you look upon the creations by Nippon workshops over the past years, especially from the Tokyo metropolitan area, the motivation of those in charge at BMW Motorrad is immediately apparent. Japanese customizing has brought forth countless sophisticated, one-of-a-kind motorcycles. From the combination of traditional Japanese craftsmanship and classic US customizing, exciting new ideas have emerged, giving the customizers of this island nation a top position within the scene.

Polite and reserved, the four Japanese men enquire about the conditions of the project. They do not want a competition where everyone is stepping into the ring against each other. It is much more important to them to showcase the four customized bikes together and to illustrate just how customizing is done in Japan. In only four months, these staggering, one-off machines, built by the country's most creative minds, will embark on a world tour.

Kaichiroh Kurosu already has some initial ideas for his customization swirling around in his head. The regular winner of "Best of Show" trophies in his home country founded Cherry's Company in 2000 and has since built many remarkable custom bikes. Kurosu's motorcycles are usually sport motorcycles. "Run, stop, and turn are the basic

CHERRY'S COMPANY
HIGHWAY FIGHTER

Februar 2014. Auf einem Sofa und ein paar Sesseln sitzen sich vier japanische Bike-Builder gegenüber, flankiert von einigen BMW Motorrad Mitarbeitern. Die Vier warten darauf, zum ersten Mal die neue BMW R nineT zu sehen und zu fühlen. Shiro Nakajima von 46 Works, Hidemo-Chef Hideya Togashi, Bratstyle-Mann Go Takamine und Kaichiroh Kurosu von Cherry's Company sind auf Einladung der deutschen Motorradmarke zusammengekommen, um das Konzept zu beraten, das Boxer-Bike nach eigenen Vorstellungen umzugestalten. Vier der begabtesten japanischen Customizer. Jeder ein eigenes Bike. Das „Project Japan".

Betrachtet man die Kreationen von Nippon-Werkstätten aus den vergangenen Jahren, vor allem aus dem Großraum Tokio, dann wird die Motivation der BMW Verantwortlichen schnell klar. Japanisches Customizing hat unzählige ausgefeilte Motorradunikate hervorgebracht. Aus der Kombination traditioneller japanischer Handwerkskunst mit klassischem US-Customizing sind spannende neue Ideen entstanden, die den Individualisierern des Inselstaats einen Spitzenplatz innerhalb der Szene verschafft haben.

Höflich und zurückhaltend erkundigen sich die vier Japaner nach den Bedingungen des Projekts. Einen Wettbewerb, bei dem jeder gegen jeden in den Ring steigt, wollen sie nicht. Ihnen liegt es viel näher, die vier umgebauten Bikes gemeinsam zu präsentieren und so zu zeigen, wie japanisches Customizing funktioniert. In nur vier Monaten sollen die atemberaubenden Unikate um die Welt reisen, gebaut von den kreativsten Köpfen des Kaiserreichs.

Im Kopf von Kaichiroh Kurosu schwirren bereits früh erste Umbauideen herum. Der Dauerabonnent auf „Best of Show"-Pokale in seiner Heimat hat die Firma Cherry's Company im Jahr 2000 gegründet und seither viele außergewöhnliche Custombikes gebaut. Meist sind die Motorräder von Kurosu sportlich. „Run, stop and turn sind die

KAICHIROH KUROSU:
“I WANT TO SHOW WHAT BMW MOTORCYCLES COULD LOOK LIKE IN TEN YEARS’ TIME.”
KAICHIROH KUROSU:
„ICH MöCHTE ZEIGEN, WIE BMW MOTORRÄDER IN ZEHN JAHREN AUSSEHEN KöNNTEN.“

"RUN, STOP, AND TURN ARE THE BASIC ELEMENTS OF EVERY MOTORCYCLE"

„RUN, STOP AND TURN SIND DIE WESENTLICHEN ELEMENTE JEDES BIKES"

METZELER
METZELER

elements of every motorcycle," Kurosu grins. However, the Highway Fighter, on the basis of the R nineT, will be much more than simply a dynamic motorcycle. Instead, Kurosu is venturing to look into the future of the motorcycle with his project. "I want to show what BMW motorcycles could look like in ten years' time." He adds: "If the engine in the bike were to be replaced with an electric motor, it wouldn't have a bad impact on the style of the bike. That is what I had in mind when I was designing it."

For this reason, Kurosu hammered out an aluminum body by hand that smoothly and harmoniously connects to all other components. The customizer is surprisingly influenced by the past: most notably, by the legendary BMW R 7 from 1934. "The line of the bike is the thing I particularly concentrated on," he recounts. "In order that all the parts would come together as a unified whole, I worked to create a single body, bringing the tank, fenders, and cowl all together, so that they didn't stand alone." In order to define the curves and corners, he extends a line along the motorcycle until he has found the perfect silhouette. He also places much of the value in his work on the details. He uses individually-cast parts as valve covers, crafts a matching silencer, carefully hides the headlight and tail light in the aluminum fairing and installs the telescopic fork of a BMW S 1000 RR and filled-in wheel rims by CCI. The former chief designer of BMW Motorrad, Ola Stenegard, sums it up nicely: "This is like a future vision, but from the past."

"My idea was to make the bike into something sportier and more aggressive," Kurosu reveals. "I think that in the end I have created something that is still a BMW at heart. This was something that I kept in the forefront of my mind, namely that this was a BMW bike and that I couldn't eliminate that BMW feel."

wesentlichen Elemente jedes Bikes", grinst der Japaner. Doch der Highway Fighter auf Basis der R nineT soll viel mehr werden als nur ein dynamisches Motorrad. Vielmehr wagt Kurosu mit seinem Projekt einen Blick in die Zukunft des Motorrads. „Ich möchte zeigen, wie BMW Motorräder in zehn Jahren aussehen könnten." Er ergänzt: „Das Design muss selbst dann funktionieren, wenn das Boxer-Aggregat gegen einen Elektromotor ausgetauscht würde."

Aus diesem Grund dengelt Kurosu von Hand einen Aluminiumbody, der alle Bauteile fließend und harmonisch miteinander verbindet. Beeinflusst wird der Customizer überraschenderweise von der Vergangenheit: von der legendären BMW R 7 von 1934. „Ich habe mich vor allem auf die Linie des Motorrads konzentriert", erzählt er, „sodass alle Komponenten – Tank, Heck und Verkleidung – als ein großes Ganzes erscheinen." Um die Kurven und Kanten zu bestimmen, richtet er so lange einen Draht entlang des Motorrads aus, bis er die perfekte Silhouette gefunden hat. Zudem legt er bei seiner Arbeit viel Wert auf Details. Er verwendet gegossene Einzelstücke als Ventildeckel, fertigt einen passenden Schalldämpfer, versteckt Scheinwerfer und Rücklicht sorgfältig in der Aluverkleidung, verbaut die Telegabel einer BMW S 1000 RR sowie geschlossene Scheibenräder von CCI. Der ehemalige Design-Chef von BMW Motorrad, Ola Stenegard, bringt es auf den Punkt: „Hey, das ist eine Zukunftsvision aus der Vergangenheit!"

„Mein Plan ist aufgegangen, das Bike deutlich sportlicher und aggressiver auszurichten als das Basismotorrad," verrät Kurosu. „Es muss jedoch immer erkennbar bleiben, dass es sich um eine BMW handelt. Dieser Gedanke spielt eine große Rolle: Ich will unbedingt das BMW Gefühl erhalten."

BRATTY'S
RNINET

GET!

Brat

THE BIKE SHOP

BRATSTYLE
CYCLONE

CUSTOMIZER	BRATSTYLE
ESTABLISHED	1998
LOCATED	TOKYO, JAPAN / LONG BEACH, CA, USA
INFO	WWW.BRATSTYLE.COM

BRATSTYLE CYCLONE

BratStyle. Isn't that the customizing workshop in Tokyo? Or does Go Takamine, founder and boss, tinker away in Long Beach, California? Both are correct. By operating in two locations, Takamine is following in the footsteps of his fellow countryman Shige Suganuma, who himself enjoys success selling his legendary Mooneyes custom parts in both Yokohama, Japan and Santa Fe Springs near Los Angeles. As early as 1998, when he opened up his tiny bike building operation in the northern Japanese city, Takamine dreamed of seeing the big wide world. Of palm trees, sunshine and wide streets crowded with surfer kids, dune buggies and custom bikes. In a word: California.

But first, this creative mind from Japan made a name for himself with his unusual bike conversions, most of which were based on Japanese mid-range motorcycles. BratStyle bikes claimed their stake thanks to their trimmed forks, short shock dampers, high-wall classic tires, and small fuel tanks. The junior mechanic combined a vintage look with distinct lightness. He borrowed a few style features from motocross and meshed them with the bobber attitude. The design was that of an American tracker with a traditional Japanese shape and feel. On the international scene, this extraordinary style made such a tremendous impact that the BratStyle concept served as the typification of a radical low-slung conversion style. It wasn't long before Go Takamine was considered one of the most influential customizers throughout Japan. Everyone was talking about BratStyle.

This level of success only intensified Takamine's longing for his dream location: southern California. He decided to satisfy this longing by opening a second shop in coastal Long Beach. The shop in Tokyo is still in operation, but this world traveler spends as much time as he can at his U.S. spot. Just as Takamine was making moves to the U.S., BMW Motorrad requested that his company create one of the four R nineT for "Project

BRATSTYLE CYCLONE

BratStyle. Ist das nicht die Customizing-Werkstatt aus Tokio? Oder schraubt Gründer und Chef Go Takamine in Long Beach, Kalifornien? Beides ist richtig. Nach dem Vorbild seines Landsmanns Shige Suganuma, der sowohl im japanischen Yokohama als auch in Santa Fe Springs bei Los Angeles erfolgreich seine legendären Mooneyes-Custom-Parts vertreibt, fährt auch Takamine zweigleisig. Bereits 1998, als er eine kleine Schrauberbude im Norden der japanischen Hauptstadt eröffnete, träumte er von der großen weiten Welt. Von Palmen, von Sonne, von breiten Straßen voller Surfer-Kids, Strandbuggys und Custombikes, kurz: von Kalifornien.

Doch zunächst einmal machte sich der kreative Japaner einen Namen mit seinen ausgefallenen Umbauten – meist auf Basis japanischer Mittelklassemotorräder. BratStyle-Bikes überraschten mit gekappten Gabeln, kurzen Stoßdämpfern, hochflankigen Classic-Reifen und kleinen Benzintanks. Der Nachwuchsmechaniker kombinierte Vintage-Look mit ausgeprägter Leichtigkeit, Bobber-Attitüde mit Motocross-Anleihen, amerikanisches Tracker-Design mit traditionellem japanischen Formgefühl. In der internationalen Szene schlug dieser außergewöhnliche Stil dermaßen ein, dass der Begriff BratStyle sogar als Typisierung für einen radikal-flachen Umbaustil herhalten musste. Schon bald galt Go Takamine als einer der einflussreichsten Customizer Japans. BratStyle war in aller Munde.

Mit dem Erfolg wuchs auch das Verlangen nach dem Sehnsuchtsort Southern California. Also erfüllte sich Takamine den Traum und eröffnete eine „Zweigstelle“ im Küstenort Long Beach. Das Ladengeschäft in Tokio besteht weiterhin, aber der Weltenbummler hält sich so oft es geht in den USA auf. Exakt auf die Zeit des Umzugs fiel auch die Anfrage von BMW Motorrad, eine der vier R nineT für das „Project Japan“ zu fertigen. Takamine musste nicht lange überlegen, ließ sich doch sein BratStyle problemlos auch auf die Heritage-BMW übertragen. „Ich überlegte mir einen flachen

GO TAKAMINE DREAMED OF SEEING THE BIG WIDE WORLD.

GO TAKAMINE TRÄUMTE VON DER GROSSEN WEITEN WELT.

BRATSTYLE'S CYCLONE IS BAVARIAN, AMERICAN, AND JAPANESE ALL AT ONCE.

DIE CYCLONE VON BRATSTYLE IST EINE US-JAPANISCHE BAYERIN.

Japan." He didn't need much time to decide. After all, his BratStyle would be very easy to apply to the Heritage BMW. "What I had in mind would be a flat dirt track, with the bike basically being used for riding the asphalt streets," says the Japanese designer. He started by focusing on parallel lines: "That would not look unusual if the bike were to be lined up with bikes that we normally deal with at BratStyle."

To ensure that the "modern day tracker" theme could be implemented, he decided on using a classic telescopic fork from Ceriani, spoke wheels with a diameter of 19 inches up front and 18 inches at the rear, and Allstate tires with a traditional profile. In the front wheel, he swapped out the twin disc brake for a duplex drum brake, achieving the perfect '70s look. Takamine smirks and says, "Although at first it looks like an older bike, I think I have achieved an interesting feel that mixes both new and old." It's not until you take a second, more discerning look that you notice the many carefully crafted details on the bike, which is Bavarian, American, and Japanese all at once. Takamine poured the front cover of the motor from aluminum with his own two hands. He also constructed the conical 2-into-2 exhaust, adapted the small fuel tank and the hump seat, and created his own custom footrest system.

According to Takamine, it mostly came down to what felt right. He says that he developed the shape intuitively and that his instinct told him that the end result would come together perfectly. When asked what location was more fitting for his Cyclone R nineT (as it came to be named) between Tokyo and Long Beach, he hesitated a bit before saying, "I did most of the building in Japan. But I would like to run it in L.A. County."

Dirt-Track-Style, vorrangig gedacht für den Einsatz auf Asphalt", erläutert der Japaner seine ersten Ideen. Zunächst konzentrierte er sich auf parallele Linien: „Das ist nicht weiter ungewöhnlich, wenn man sich die Motorräder anschaut, die bei BratStyle normalerweise entstehen."

Um das Thema eines Modern-Day-Trackers umsetzen zu können, entschied er sich für die Verwendung einer klassischen Teleskopgabel von Ceriani für Speichenräder mit vorne 19 Zoll, hinten 18 Zoll Durchmesser und Allstate-Reifen mit traditionellem Profil. Im Vorderrad ersetzte er die Doppelscheibenbremse gegen eine Duplex-Trommelbremse und erzielte so den perfekten Seventies-Look. Go Takamine grinst: „Auf den ersten Blick sieht sie aus wie eine ältere Maschine. Ich denke, ich habe einen interessanten Mix aus Alt und Neu geschaffen." Erst auf den zweiten, genaueren Blick entdeckt der Betrachter die vielen sorgfältig ausgeführten Details an der US-japanischen Bayerin. So hat Takamine den Stirndeckel des Motors eigenhändig aus Aluminium gegossen, den konischen 2-in-2-Auspuff angefertigt, den kleinen Benzintank sowie die Höckersitzbank angepasst und eine individuelle Fußrastenanlage konstruiert.

Vor allem auf ein gutes Gefühl sei es ihm angekommen, erzählt Go Takamine. Er habe die Form intuitiv entwickelt und sein Gespür sage ihm, dass das Ergebnis durchaus gelungen sei. Auf die Frage, an welchen Ort denn seine Cyclone genannte R nineT besser passe, nach Tokio oder Long Beach, antwortet er nur zögerlich: „Gebaut habe ich sie vor allem in Japan. Aber fahren möchte ich sie in L.A. County."

消火器

46works
Shiroh Nakajima

46WORKS
CLUBMAN RACER

CUSTOMIZER	46WORKS
ESTABLISHED	2014
LOCATED	YATSUGATAKE, JAPAN
INFO	46WORKS.NET

46
46works
BMW
brembo

46works
Shiroh Nakajima

46WORKS
CLUBMAN RACER

There are bike builders who slave away for days and weeks in their shops in an effort to find the perfect design for their bike projects. Many of them complete an endless amount of drawings before they pick up any tools, while others can be found visiting the hot scene spots for their craft almost every weekend, waiting for inspiration to strike. And then there are customizers like Shiro Nakajima, who do as much riding as possible on the racetracks of Japan to thoroughly test and further optimize their bikes. Thanks to a heavily modified BMW R 75/5, a picturesque R 90 S, or a Moto Guzzi racer, this Japanese builder dominates racing series such as the Legend of Classic, which takes place several times per year on the Tsukuba Circuit and the Fuji Speedway.

It's no surprise at all then, that the vast majority of bikes that leave Nakajima's company, 46Works, fit right in on the racetrack. Shiro thinks of café racer conversions as the smallest level of expansion. For him, they serve as the basis for all other modifications. His favorites are extremely lightweight racing machines that aren't street legal. Reinforced frames, optimized suspension elements, and highly capable brakes are all part of the standard repertoire for the creations brought to life by 46Works. Over the years, Shiro Nakajima has developed into a true master of technical upgrades for classic European motorcycles.

But even long before this development, BMW Motorrad had been watching the sporty activities of 46Works like a hawk. Nakajima founded the Ritmo Sereno custom shop way back in 2001 in the rooms of what used to be a car dealer in Tokyo. Lightning-fast BMW boxer engines were created there. After a few years among the hustle and bustle of the big city, the former professional musician began to yearn for a cozy rural life. Founding 46Works near the Yatsugatake mountains meant starting a new chapter. A lot changed, but Shiro's passion for fast BMW bikes remained.

In the eyes of BMW Motorrad management, this made him the perfect participant in "Project Japan." The talented bike engineer went straight to work on "his" R nineT.

46WORKS
CLUBMAN RACER

Es gibt Bike-Builder, die hocken viele Tage und Wochen in ihrer Werkstatt, um die optimale Form für ihr Bikeprojekt zu finden. Manche fertigen unzählige Zeichnungen an, bevor sie mit dem Schrauben beginnen, andere besuchen an fast jedem Wochenende einschlägige Szenetreffen, um sich inspirieren zu lassen. Und es gibt Customizer wie Shiro Nakajima, die treiben sich so oft es geht auf den Rennstrecken Japans herum, um ihre Bikes gründlich zu testen und weiter zu optimieren. Mit seiner stark modifizierten BMW R 75/5, einer bildhübschen R 90 S oder einem Moto-Guzzi-Racer dominiert der Japaner zum Beispiel die Rennserie Legend of Classic, die mehrmals im Jahr auf Strecken wie dem Tsukuba Circuit und dem Fuji Speedway stattfindet.

So verwundert es kaum, dass fast alle Bikes, die Nakajimas Firma 46Works verlassen, auf dem Racetrack zu Hause sind. Umbauten zum Cafe Racer hält Shiro für die kleinste Ausbaustufe, für die Basis aller weiteren Modifikationen. Seine Lieblinge sind federleichte Rennmaschinen ohne Straßenzulassung. Verstärkte Rahmen, optimierte Federelemente oder taugliche Bremsen zählen daher zum Standardrepertoire an den Kreationen von 46Works. Im Laufe der Jahre hat sich Shiro Nakajima zu einem wahren Meister der technischen Upgrades an klassischen europäischen Motorrädern entwickelt.

BMW Motorrad hatte das sportliche Treiben von 46Works schon länger mit großem Interesse beobachtet. Bereits in dem Customshop Ritmo-Sereno, den Nakajima 2001 in den Räumen eines ehemaligen Autohauses in Tokio gegründet hat, entstanden pfeilschnelle BMW Boxer. Nach einigen Jahren in der Hektik der Großstadt sehnte sich der ehemalige Profimusiker dann nach gemütlichem Landleben und schlug mit 46Works am Fuß des Yatsugatake-Gebirges ein neues Kapitel auf. Vieles änderte sich. Die Leidenschaft für schnelle BMW jedoch blieb erhalten.

So schien Shiro Nakajima für die Verantwortlichen von BMW Motorrad der ideale Teilnehmer am „Project Japan" zu sein. Der talentierte Techniker begann umgehend

46works
Shiro Nakajima

He focused on optimizing the suspension of the classic 1200 with Öhlins components and reducing weight. Shiro says, "I focused on aspects such as lightness, speed, and ease of operation. I would guess that it is approximately 30kg lighter than the standard R nineT, so the rider can actually feel that the bike is lighter simply by pushing it." Light wheels in the MotoGP style, low-mounted clip-on handlebars, a titanium exhaust system, and an oil cooler from Earl's round off the sporty conversion and help to "slim down" the bike design. The biggest challenge of all, however, was building the hand-made aluminum chassis. Shiro Nakajima used aluminum sheet metal to build the tank and tail section.

In the end, the head of 46Works had taken the R nineT and created something that lived up to all expectations: The lightweight Clubman Racer cuts a perfect physique on the racetrack. But Shiro sees yet another area of application for his creation: "I think I have created a bike that would be really enjoyable to ride on winding mountain roads." Mission accomplished. In spades.

mit der Arbeit an „seiner" R nineT. Er konzentrierte sich darauf, das Fahrwerk der klassischen 1200er mit Komponenten von Öhlins zu optimieren und das Gewicht zu reduzieren. Dazu Shiro: „Ich fokussierte mich auf die Aspekte Gewicht, Geschwindigkeit und leichte Handhabung. Das Motorrad ist nun etwa 30 Kilogramm leichter als das Original. Bereits beim Schieben ist das eindrucksvoll zu spüren." Leichte Räder im MotoGP Style, tief angebrachte Clip-on-Lenker, eine Titan-Auspuffanlage und ein Ölkühler von Earl's vervollständigen den Sportumbau und unterstützen die konsequente Diät. Die größte Herausforderung war jedoch die Herstellung des handgemachten Aluminiumchassis: Shiro Nakajima fertigte Tank und Heckteil selbst.

Am Ende hat der 46Works-Mann exakt das mit der R nineT angestellt, was man von ihm erwartet hatte: Auf der Rennstrecke gibt der leichte Clubman Racer eine perfekte Figur ab. Doch Shiro sieht ein weiteres Einsatzgebiet für seine Kreation: „Ich denke, ich habe ein Bike gebaut, mit dem man auf kurvigen Bergstraßen einen Riesenspaß haben kann." Auftrag mit Bravour erfüllt.

SHIRO NAKAJIMA DOES AS MUCH RIDING AS POSSIBLE ON THE RACETRACKS OF JAPAN

SHIRO NAKAJIMA TREIBT SICH SO OFT ES GEHT AUF DEN RENNSTRECKEN JAPANS HERUM

"I THINK I HAVE CREATED A BIKE THAT WOULD BE REALLY ENJOYABLE TO RIDE ON WINDING MOUNTAIN ROADS."

„ICH DENKE, ICH HABE EIN BIKE GEBAUT, MIT DEM MAN AUF KURVIGEN BERGSTRASSEN EINEN RIESENSPASS HABEN KANN."

brembo

Hide Motorcycle

HIDE MOTORCYCLE
BOXER

CUSTOMIZER	HIDE MOTORCYCLE
ESTABLISHED	2003
LOCATED	KAWASAKI, JAPAN
INFO	WWW.HIDEMO.NET

"NOT A NORMAL CUSTOM BUILD PROJECT"

„KEIN NORMALES CUSTOM-PROJEKT"

HIDE MOTORCYCLE BOXER

Trucks thunder loudly through the streets of Kawasaki towards Tokyo and compact cars hustle to position themselves to pass; all of this hardly a meter from the motorcycle blacksmiths of Hide Motorcycle's shop windows. No sidewalk, no parking bay. Hideya Togashi runs his small custom store here directly on the Tama River. Despite tight working spaces and a rather impractical layout over two floors, the cautious man weighing in at 50 kg ranks among the most popular and most innovative customizers in Japan. Among piles of spare parts, narrow steel stairs, and vibrating street noise, Hideya produces outrageously unique motorcycles and readily draws upon US basis bikes and European accessories. He combines Japanese minimalism with clean craftsmanship, creating his inimitably cool style.

Hide Motorcycle, Hidemo for short, also ranks among the chosen few to demonstrate Japanese engineering using the BMW R nineT as an example—by official order from BMW Motorrad. Hideya Togashi decides to develop a full fairing for the Heritage BMW in an effort to emphasize its dynamic side. What caused the scrupulous craftsman the most headaches was creating the aluminum tank, which was to remain raw and without a paint coat. "I would say that the tank is probably the characteristic of this bike. For this custom project I wanted to show the aluminum in its natural state, without painting it. I therefore had to beat out the shape of the aluminum tank," says Hideya in a quiet voice describing his work. Former BMW Motorrad chief designer, Ola Stenegard, understands the enormous effort: "I like that he left all the aluminum just brushed. You would see any imperfections if there were any. But there is nothing; it is just perfect."

The Hidemo boss even tactfully allows the streamlined tail section to be formed from sheet aluminum. The effort and attention to detail is typical for Hide Motorcycle; for instance the aluminum valve cover specifically cast for BMW, the ribbed cover for the

HIDE MOTORCYCLE BOXER

Lautstark donnern Lastwagen über die Straße von Kawasaki nach Tokio, Kompaktautos setzen hektisch zum Überholen an – kaum einen Meter vom Schaufenster der Motorradschmiede Hide Motorcycle entfernt. Kein Fußweg, keine Parkbucht. Hideya Togashi betreibt hier, unmittelbar am Tama River gelegen, seinen kleinen Custom Store. Trotz beengter Platzverhältnisse und der eher unpraktischen Raumaufteilung über zwei Etagen, zählt der bedächtig agierende 50-Kilo-Mann zu den angesagtesten und innovativsten Customizern Japans. Zwischen gestapelten Ersatzteilen, enger Stahltreppe und vibrierendem Straßenlärm produziert Hideya unfassbare Motorradunikate und greift dabei gerne auf US-amerikanische Basisbikes und europäisches Zubehör zurück. Er kombiniert japanischen Minimalismus mit sauberem Handwerk und kreiert daraus seinen unnachahmlich coolen Stil.

Auch Hide Motorcycle, kurz Hidemo, zählen zu den Auserwählten, die japanische Baukunst am Beispiel der BMW R nineT demonstrieren sollen – im offiziellen Auftrag von BMW Motorrad. Hideya Togashi beschließt, eine Vollverkleidung für die Heritage-BMW zu entwickeln, um ihre dynamische Seite zu betonen. Am meisten Kopfzerbrechen bereitet dem peniblen Handwerker die Herstellung des Aluminiumtanks, der roh, ohne abschließenden Lacküberzug bleiben soll. „Für mich ist der Benzintank das Erkennungsmerkmal eines Motorrads. Das Aluminium soll bei der R nineT in seiner natürlichen Beschaffenheit gezeigt werden. Daher kann ich keinen glättenden Spachtel verwenden," beschreibt Hideya seine Arbeit mit leiser Stimme. Der ehemalige BMW Motorrad-Designchef Ola Stenegard weiß um den enormen Aufwand: „Unsauber gearbeitete Stellen am Tank würden sofort ins Auge springen. Falls es denn welche geben würde. Aber die gibt es nicht, alles ist absolut perfekt."

Auch das schlanke Heckteil lässt der Hidemo-Chef mit viel Feingefühl aus Aluminiumblech entstehen. Typisch für Hide Motorcycle ist der Aufwand, der für die Details

"TO GET TO THE BATTERY YOU FLIP UP THE TAIL, AND IT DOES NOT JUST GO 'CLONK' UP; YOU JUST DROP IT DOWN AND IT GOES 'PSHHHHHH...'. UNBELIEVABLE."

„UM AN DIE BATTERIE ZU GELANGEN, WIRD DAS HECK LAUTLOS AUFGEKLAPPT. BEIM HERUNTERLASSEN MACHT ES NUR ‚PSHHHHHH'. UNGLAUBLICH."

coils, and the elegant fluid reservoirs for the clutch and brake. First-class manufacturing with perfect function that can only be recognized as being custom parts after first glance. Hidemo installs the upside-down fork sliders from the BMW S 1000 RR super sport, flat clip-on handlebars, and an exhaust that snakes below the motor in MotoGP style. Ola Stenegard is excited by the workmanship of the Hidemo-nineT: "To get to the battery you flip up the tail, and it does not just go 'clonk' up, like on a modern car; you just drop it down and it goes 'pshhhhhh...'. So it is just so well-built on every level, unbelievable."

Hideya Togashi is pleased with the recognition from the BMW design department and promptly returns the favor: "It's already a very stylish and good-looking bike without being customized, so the challenge is to consider what you can improve or how you can make it look better with a custom build." Outside the window, a tanker truck rattles on by. The slender gearhead has to speak a bit more loudly: "That is the concept I was working from for this project and in that sense I don't think that it has been a normal custom build project."

betrieben wird, etwa die speziell für die BMW gegossenen Alu-Ventildeckel, gerippte Cover für die Zündspulen und die eleganten Flüssigkeitsbehälter für Kupplung und Bremse. Edel verarbeitet, mit perfekter Funktion und erst auf den zweiten Blick als Custom-Parts erkennbar. Hidemo verbaut die Upside-down-Gabel des Supersportlers BMW S 1000 RR, flache Clip-on-Lenker und einen unter dem Motor platzierten Auspuff im MotoGP-Style. Ola Stenegard zeigt sich begeistert von der Verarbeitungsqualität der Hidemo-nineT: „Um an die Batterie zu gelangen, wird das Heck lautlos wie die Haube an einem modernen Auto aufgeklappt. Beim Herunterlassen macht es nur ‚pshhhhhh'. Unglaublich. Die Verarbeitungsqualität befindet sich auf einem extrem hohen Level."

Hideya Togashi freut sich über die Anerkennung aus der BMW Designabteilung und revanchiert sich prompt: „Bereits vor dem Umbau war die R nineT ein gut aussehendes und stylishes Bike. Die Herausforderung bestand darin, etwas zu finden, was dennoch verbessert werden kann." Draußen vor der Scheibe rattert ein Tanklastzug vorbei. Der feingliedrige Schrauber muss etwas lauter sprechen: „Nein, für mich war das kein normales Custom-Projekt."

HIDEYA TOGASHI COMBINES JAPANESE MINIMALISM WITH CLEAN CRAFTSMANSHIP, CREATING HIS INIMITABLY COOL STYLE.

HIDEYA TOGASHI KOMBINIERT JAPANISCHEN MINIMALISMUS MIT SAUBEREM HANDWERK UND KREIERT DARAUS SEINEN UNNACHAHMLICH COOLEN STIL.

THE CHOSEN FEW DEMONSTRATE JAPANESE ENGINEERING USING THE BMW R NINE T AS AN EXAMPLE

DIE AUSERWÄHLTEN DEMONSTRIEREN JAPANISCHE BAUKUNST AM BEISPIEL DER R NINE T

BMW
brembo

ROUGH CRAFTS

ROUGH CRAFTS
BAVARIAN FISTFIGHTER

CUSTOMIZER	ROUGH CRAFTS
ESTABLISHED	2010
LOCATED	TAIPEI, TAIWAN
INFO	WWW.ROUGHCRAFTS.COM

“AND EVERY PART WAS MADE IN TAIWAN.”

„UND DAS ALLES IST MADE IN TAIWAN.“

ROUGH CRAFTS BAVARIAN FISTFIGHTER

Winston Yeh is among the world's most recognizable up-and-comers in the custom bike scene. This is surprising to hear at first, since his bike shop is located in Taipei, the capital of Taiwan. It's hard to imagine anyone making cool custom bikes so popular in that small island nation. But according to Winston, "Taipei probably has the most motorcycles and scooters per square kilometer." It also has a small—yet excellent—modification culture that is gradually gaining traction. This is because more and more residents of Taiwan are beginning to enjoy an individualistic lifestyle that takes on the Western example. Custom bikes are being brought into fashion.

This makes it important for the resourceful gearhead to set the record straight on the reputation of his home country. "There are all kinds of motorcycle accessories being produced here. Products made in Taiwan can't really be compared with cheap products from other Asian countries," says Winston boldly as he shows off a high-quality milled part of his own making. And thanks to his exceptional bike creations, each of which bears an inimitable signature style, Taiwan is considered among the world's elite when it comes to customizing.

In 2010, the young bike builder started running his own workshop in Ximen, a trendy shopping neighborhood of Taipei. He went to bike shows in Europe and America as a lone wolf, competing with confidence under the trademark "Made in Taiwan." Only three years later, he won the "World Championship of Custom Bike Building," and in 2014 he received the "Best of Show" award at the Custombike Show in Bad Salzuflen, Germany. Rough Crafts motorcycles are almost always black with a very clean look, based on motorcycles currently in production. Unlike many other international bike builders, vintage bikes and classics don't really do it for Winston. It wasn't surprising at all that BMW Motorrad took notice of the graduate in Industrial Design, and they offered him the thrilling opportunity to take part in the Soul Fuel project.

Winston was completely taken by the notion of building his own interpretation of the R nineT: the Bavarian Fistfighter. He had a concept for a modern and sporty bike that told a powerful story about the brand with the blue and white emblem. "The Bavarian Fistfighter is a tribute to the past, mixed with modern technology," says Winston. He went straight to work, producing special parts for the BMW. He designed a bulbous tank from aluminum sheet that evokes the twin-valve boxer models of the

ROUGH CRAFTS BAVARIAN FISTFIGHTER

Winston Yeh zählt zu den international anerkanntesten Nachwuchs-Customizern. Das erstaunt zunächst, denn seine kleine Manufaktur befindet sich in Taipeh, der Hauptstadt von Taiwan. Wohl kaum jemand bringt den kleinen Inselstaat in Verbindung mit coolen Custombikes. Doch nach Aussagen von Winston existieren in Taipeh vielleicht die meisten Motorräder und Scooter pro Quadratkilometer. Auch eine kleine, aber feine Umbauszene wächst langsam heran. Denn mehr und mehr findet man auch in Taiwan Gefallen an einer individuellen Lebensweise nach westlichem Vorbild. Custombikes kommen schwer in Mode.

Für den findigen Schrauber ist es daher besonders wichtig, den Ruf seiner Heimat ins rechte Licht zu rücken. „Bei uns wird jede Menge Zubehör für Motorräder gefertigt. Produkte aus Taiwan sind nicht zu vergleichen mit Billigartikeln aus anderen asiatischen Ländern." Winston zeigt überzeugt ein hochwertig verarbeitetes Frästeil aus eigener Fertigung. Und dank seiner ausgefallenen Bike-Kreationen, die stets eine unnachahmliche Handschrift tragen, zählt Taiwan beim Thema Customizing mittlerweile zur Weltspitze.

2010 startete der Nachwuchs-Bike-Builder mit seiner eigenen Werkstatt in Ximen, einem Einkaufs- und Szeneviertel von Taipeh. Er tingelte als Einzelkämpfer zu europäischen und amerikanischen Bikeshows und warb selbstbewusst mit dem Markenzeichen „Made in Taiwan". Bereits drei Jahre später räumte er die „World Championship of Custombike Building" ab, und 2014 erhielt er für eine seiner Kreationen den „Best of Show"-Award auf der Custombike Show in Bad Salzuflen. Die Motorräder von Rough Crafts sind fast immer schwarz, sehr clean und basieren auf Motorrädern aktueller Produktion. Anders als viele seiner internationalen Kollegen kann Winston mit Vintage Bikes und Oldtimern nicht viel anfangen. So verwundert es kaum, dass BMW Motorrad auf den diplomierten Industrial Designer aufmerksam wurde, um ihn für das Projekt Soul Fuel zu begeistern.

Winston war fasziniert von der Idee, eine eigene Interpretation der R nineT zu bauen, einen Bavarian Fistfighter. Ihm schwebte ein modernes, sportliches Motorrad vor, das die Geschichte der weiß-blauen Marke überzeugend zitiert. „Eine Verbeugung vor der Vergangenheit, angereichert mit aktueller Technologie", bringt es der junge Taiwanese auf den Punkt. Also begann er damit, spezielle Teile für die BMW anzufertigen. Er

1970s based on its dark paint job and classic double stripes. In addition, he created a leather solo seat in the style of the classic rubber seats and designed aluminum cast wheels in the “snowflake” design of the /7 models from BMW. “The rear 17-inch wheel has a sturdy 6 inch width,” reports Winston.

To add some pronounced contrast to the traditional shapes, Winston used Beringer hand brakes, a Gears Racing strut, a case cover from Roland Sands Design, and Pirelli racing tires. He created exhaust systems and suction heads as one-off parts for the Bavarian Fistfighter with his own hands. This left the engine and gears as the only remaining original parts: “110 bhp is all you need.” To tie together the overall look, he hid the electronic components neatly below the tank. “It ought to look simple even if it’s anything but,” says Winston.

“BMW Motorrad is a brand with a rich history, and one of Rough Crafts’ main design aesthetics is to blend the beautiful lines from the past with modern finishes.” Winston Yeh proudly takes in his Bavarian Fistfighter and says, “And every part was made in Taiwan.”

kreierte einen bauchigen Tank aus Aluminiumblech, der mit einer dunklen Lackierung und traditionellen Doppelstreifen an die Zweiventil-Boxermodelle der 1970er-Jahre erinnert. Weiterhin schuf er einen Solositz aus Leder im Stil klassischer Gummisättel und er entwarf Aluminiumgussräder im „Schneeflocken“-Design der „Strich-Sieben“-Modelle von BMW. „Das hintere 17-Zoll-Rad hat eine Breite von mächtigen 6 Zoll“, verrät Winston.

Im krassen Kontrast zu den traditionellen Formen stehen die Beringer-Handarmaturen, das Federbein von Gears Racing, die Gehäusedeckel von Roland Sands Design und die Pirelli-Rennreifen. Auspuffanlage und Ansaugtrichter hat Winston als Unikate für den Bavarian Fistfighter eigenhändig angefertigt. Original beließ er lediglich Motor und Getriebe: „110 PS reichen völlig.“ Um ein harmonisches Ganzes zu erzielen, versteckte er die elektronischen Komponenten geschickt unter dem Tank. „Es soll einfach aussehen, auch wenn es definitiv alles andere als das ist“, sagt Winston.

„BMW Motorrad ist eine Marke mit reicher Geschichte. Als vorrangiges Designmerkmal habe ich die Formensprache der Vergangenheit mit modernem Finish vereint.“ Voller Stolz blickt Winston Yeh auf seinen bayerischen Faustkämpfer: „Und das alles ist made in Taiwan.“

“THE BAVARIAN FIST-FIGHTER IS A TRIBUTE TO THE PAST, MIXED WITH MODERN TECHNOLOGY.”

„EINE VERBEUGUNG VOR DER VERGANGENHEIT, ANGEREICHERT MIT AKTUELLER TECHNOLOGIE“

BMW
brembo

Church

CHURCH OF CHOPPERS
COC R NINE T

CUSTOMIZER	CHURCH OF CHOPPERS
ESTABLISHED	1995
LOCATED	DES MOINES, IA, USA
INFO	WWW.CHURCHOFCHOPPERS.COM

JEFF ONLY WORKS ON BIKES THAT HE PERSONALLY LIKES.

JEFF BAUT AUSSCHLIESSLICH DAS, WAS IHM PERSÖNLICH GEFÄLLT.

CHURCH OF CHOPPERS
COC R NINE T

He's a pub keeper, owner of the FTWCO fashion label and devoted father to his three children. In his spare time, Jeff Wright has been reporting on the international bike customization culture in his blog, Church of Choppers, since 2011. Incidentally, he also frequently designs and builds eclectic one-of-a-kind motorcycles. It's no wonder that this tireless customizer with limitless talent rarely goes to bed before four o'clock in the morning.

At his workbench in Des Moines, Iowa, he tinkers with bikes from a variety of manufacturers and styles: Classics, choppers, streetfighters, dirt trackers. No bike is safe from the bold ingenuity of Wright, who holds a degree in art. And Jeff only works on bikes that he personally likes. "What I tell people is this: If you like something I've built, make me an offer. But I won't build a bike for anyone other than myself."

In late 2015, when he was asked by BMW Motorrad if he wanted to convert an R nineT, he spontaneously agreed. He was sure he could pencil in a new project for sometime after midnight. "I live in the middle of the USA. When you live 2,000 miles from California and 1,500 miles from New York City, it's great to get a chance to exercise your creativity on a bike like this," says Jeff, thankful for the opportunity.

The blogger, gearhead, and pub keeper took the boxer-based BMW bike and turned it into a true masterpiece. Jeff's trademark style involves designing all of his bikes to be as minimalist as possible. He refers to this method as "cleaning up" with a slightly furrowed brow. The R nineT was no exception. His plan was to get rid of as much clutter as possible. To this end, he removed the installed on-board electronics including the fuel injection system and replaced them with two classic flat side carburetors. This expert on the custom bike scene also relied on unconventional solutions for the ignition system. Instead of an electronic map-controlled ignition, he installed a

CHURCH OF CHOPPERS
COC R NINE T

Er ist Kneipenwirt, Inhaber des Modelabels FTWCO und treu sorgender Familienvater für seine drei Kids. Außerdem verbreitet Jeff Wright seit 2011 in seinem Blog Church of Choppers News aus der internationalen Customszene. Und ganz nebenbei entwickelt und baut er regelmäßig stilbildende Motorrad-Unikate. Kein Wunder, dass das rastlose Universaltalent nur selten vor vier Uhr morgens ins Bett fällt.

Auf seiner Werkbank in Des Moines, der Hauptstadt von Iowa, tummeln sich Bikes unterschiedlichster Hersteller und Stile: Klassiker, Chopper, Streetfighter, Dirt Tracker. Kaum ein Motorrad ist vor der Bastelwut des studierten Kunstwissenschaftlers sicher. Und Jeff baut ausschließlich das, was ihm persönlich gefällt. „Ich sage den Leuten: Wenn Du etwas magst, was ich gebaut habe, dann mach mir ein Angebot. Ich werde kein Motorrad für jemanden anderes bauen als für mich selbst."

Als er Ende 2015 von BMW Motorrad gefragt wird, ob er eine R nineT umbauen will, sagt er spontan zu. Irgendwann nach Mitternacht wird sich schon noch Zeit für ein neues Projekt finden. „Ich lebe in der Mitte der USA, und bei 2.000 Meilen bis Kalifornien und 1.500 Meilen bis New York City ist es toll, eine Chance zu bekommen, an so einem Bike herumzubasteln", bedankt sich Jeff für diese Gelegenheit.

Also nahm sich der Blogger, Schrauber und Gastronom der Boxer-BMW an und schuf ein wahres Meisterwerk. Jeffs Markenzeichen ist es, alle seine Bikes so minimalistisch wie möglich zu gestalten. „Aufräumen" nennt er diese Vorgehensweise mit leicht mürrischem Gesichtsausdruck. Auch bei der R nineT wollte er soviel Ballast abwerfen wie möglich. Dazu entfernte er die verbaute Bordelektronik inklusive der Einspritzanlage und ersetzte diese durch zwei klassische Flachschiebervergaser. Auch bei der Zündanlage vertraute der Szenekenner auf ungewöhnliche Lösungen. Statt einer elektronischen Kennfeldzündung verbaute er einen traditionellen Magnetzünder.

agv
brembo

“WHAT JEFF HAS ACCOMPLISHED HERE IS SPECTACULAR.”

„WAS JEFF DA GESCHAFFEN HAT, IST SPEKTAKULÄR.“

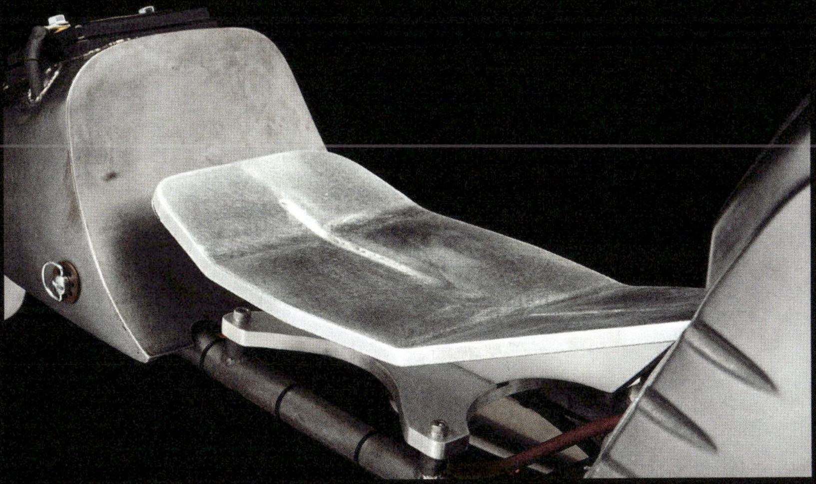

traditional magneto. The on-board battery needs to be regularly connected to a charger to supply electrical consumers like blinkers or the horn, making it all the more practical that the poles of the battery (installed in a recess in the seat hump) be easily accessible.

Jeff stripped the black paint from the frame and had it anodized at a specialist facility. The round headlight on the front had to be scrapped, and the delicate hump seat makes it clear to see that the design is light and unfettered by bells and whistles. Racing slicks were added to make the 1200cc bike ready for the racetrack. When reporting on his BMW conversion, Jeff spoke pensively and carefully, saying "I can recall how much I enjoyed putting the parts of this bike together. It was a design that required a lot of care." The American designer paid a great deal of attention to the exhaust system. The two twisted manifold lines lead to two tiny, stylish mufflers ending under the seat and positioned at an unconventional 30-degree angle to each other.

"What Jeff has accomplished here is spectacular," says Christian Pingitzer, Head of Sales and Marketing Strategy Heritage & Customizing at BMW Motorrad. "Of course, fuel injection is typically the way to go when pure performance is a concern. But the bike looks great, is lightweight, fast, and has one hell of a powerful sound!"

IN THE INITIAL STAGE, THE MOTORCYCLE DID NOT NEED ANY PAINT AT ALL. TWO MONTHS LATER, THE PAINT SHOP PROVIDED RAZOR-SHARP DETAILING.

IM ERSTEN STADIUM KAM DIE MASCHINE NOCH VÖLLIG OHNE FARBE AUS. ZWEI MONATE SPÄTER SETZTE DIE LACKIERUNG PUNKTGENAUE AKZENTE.

Zur Versorgung der elektrischen Verbraucher wie Blinker oder Hupe muss die Bordbatterie regelmäßig an ein Ladegerät. Wie praktisch, dass die Pole des im Sitzbankhöcker versenkten Akkus schnell zugänglich sind.

Jeff entfernte die schwarze Lackierung vom Rahmen und ließ ihn in einem Fachbetrieb hochglänzend eloxieren. Der Rundscheinwerfer an der Front musste weichen, und eine filigrane Höckersitzbank verdeutlicht bereits optisch die Leichtigkeit des luftigen Entwurfs. Slickbereifung soll die 1200er zudem renntauglich machen. Im ersten Stadium kam die Maschine noch völlig ohne Farbe aus. Zwei Monate später setzte die Lackierung punktgenaue Akzente. „Ich erinnere mich daran, wie toll ich es fand, das Motorrad zusammenzubauen. Eine sehr sorgfältige Entwicklung", meint Jeff rückblickend. Besonderes Augenmerk verwendete der Amerikaner auf die Auspuffanlage. Die beiden verschlungenen Krümmer münden in zwei winzigen, frech unter der Sitzbank endenden Schalldämpfern, die zudem im ungewöhnlichen 30-Grad-Winkel zueinander stehen.

„Was Jeff da geschaffen hat, ist spektakulär", sagt Christian Pingitzer, Marketing-Mann für Heritage und Customizing bei BMW Motorrad. „Natürlich ist die Kraftstoffeinspritzung meist eine bessere Wahl, wenn es um reine Performance geht. Doch die Maschine sieht super aus, ist leicht, schnell und hat einen infernalischen Sound."

JVB MOTO
NINE T SCRAMBLER

CUSTOMIZER	JVB MOTO
ESTABLISHED	2001
LOCATED	HÜRTH, GERMANY
INFO	WWW.JVB-MOTO.COM

JVB MOTO
NINE T SCRAMBLER

Parked behind a giant puddle are wide-tired cars, owned by the customers of an American car repair shop. Through the open door of a vintage resale shop, you can see a flash of orange plastic furniture. Right next door is the large industrial building in which, until recently, designer Jens vom Brauck concocted his concepts and finished his two-wheeled masterpieces. Full of nooks and crannies, the complex of brick buildings is part of an old paint factory right on the banks of the Rhine, overlooking the Zoo Bridge in Cologne. Behind the two-part gray steel door, the head of JvB Moto devised a very special BMW R nineT. Only after its completion did his company move to a new location in Hürth, south of Cologne. "Now we're in a state-of-the-art industrial building with in-floor heating," says Jens with a grin.

However, he had modified the first R nineT Scrambler in the halls of the old factory. He is one of three customizers that BMW Motorrad charged with the task of converting a scrambler for the project Soul Fuel. "I don't just rebuild a motorcycle," says Jens, explaining his methodology. "For each design, I need a topic, a direction. A motorcycle has to look the same as it feels." On that point, the designer has mastered a knack for always giving the bike a touch of wear and tear—ratty and cool. Vom Brauck knows exactly how to draw out a motorcycle's classic aura. In each project, he adapts his minimalistic design language to every bike he works on.

The design "sculptor" first develops his creations using software, then draws them out on paper. Only later are designs made from clay, hard foam or fiberglass formed on the motorcycle at a scale of 1:1. "I've also attempted a few designs on smaller models," says Jens. The usual outcome of this process features stable, multi-piece molds for part reproduction. "For individual pieces, a positive mold often suffices," he says, pointing to the BMW headlight mask. Aluminum parts such as the streamlined rear part of the scrambler are also shaped and welded by the self-made man himself.

JVB MOTO
NINE T SCRAMBLER

Hinter einer riesigen Pfütze parken die breitbereiften Kundenfahrzeuge eines US-Car-Schraubers und durch die offene Tür eines Antiquitätenhändlers blitzen orangefarbene Kunststoffmöbel. Gleich nebenan befindet sich auch die Halle, in der Designer Jens vom Brauck bis vor Kurzem seine Ideen ausgebrütet und seine zweirädrigen Meisterstücke vollendet hat. Die verwinkelten Backsteingebäude sind Teil einer ehemaligen Farbenfabrik, unmittelbar am Rheinufer, mit Blick auf die Zoobrücke in Köln. Hinter dem grauen, doppelflügeligen Stahltor hat der Kopf von JvB Moto eine ganz besondere BMW R nineT erdacht. Erst nach deren Fertigstellung ist er samt seiner Firma nach Hürth, südlich von Köln, gezogen. „In eine moderne Gewerbehalle – mit Fußbodenheizung", so Jens grinsend.

Den ersten Umbau der R nineT Scrambler hat er jedoch noch in den alten Hallen durchgeführt. Er ist einer von drei Customizern, die mit der Gestaltung einer Scrambler für das Projekt Soul Fuel von BMW Motorrad beauftragt wurden. „Ich baue ein Motorrad nicht einfach um", erklärt Jens seine Vorgehensweise. „Für jeden Entwurf brauche ich ein Thema, eine Richtung. Denn ein Motorrad muss aussehen, wie es sich anfühlt." Dazu beherrscht der Designer den Kniff, ein Bike stets ein wenig abgerockt und lässig wirken zu lassen. Vom Brauck weiß ganz genau, wie er die klassische Ausstrahlung eines Motorrads herauskitzeln kann. Seine minimalistische Formensprache passt er stets auf das jeweilige Fahrzeug an.

Der Formgestalter entwickelt seine Kreationen zunächst am Rechner, dann zeichnet er sie auf Papier, erst später entstehen Entwürfe aus der Modelliermasse Clay, aus Hartschaum oder GfK am Motorrad in 1:1. „Einige Designs habe ich auch an kleinen Modellen erprobt", erzählt Jens. Im Anschluss entstehen stabile, mehrteilige Formen, um die Parts reproduzieren zu können. „Für Einzelstücke genügt mir oft auch eine Positivform", und zeigt auf die Lampenmaske der BMW. Aluminiumteile wie das schlanke Heckteil des Scramblers formt und schweißt der Selfmade-Mann ebenfalls selbst.

"I DON'T JUST REBUILD
A MOTORCYCLE."
„ICH BAUE EIN MOTOR-
RAD NICHT EINFACH UM."

one

NINET
R1200

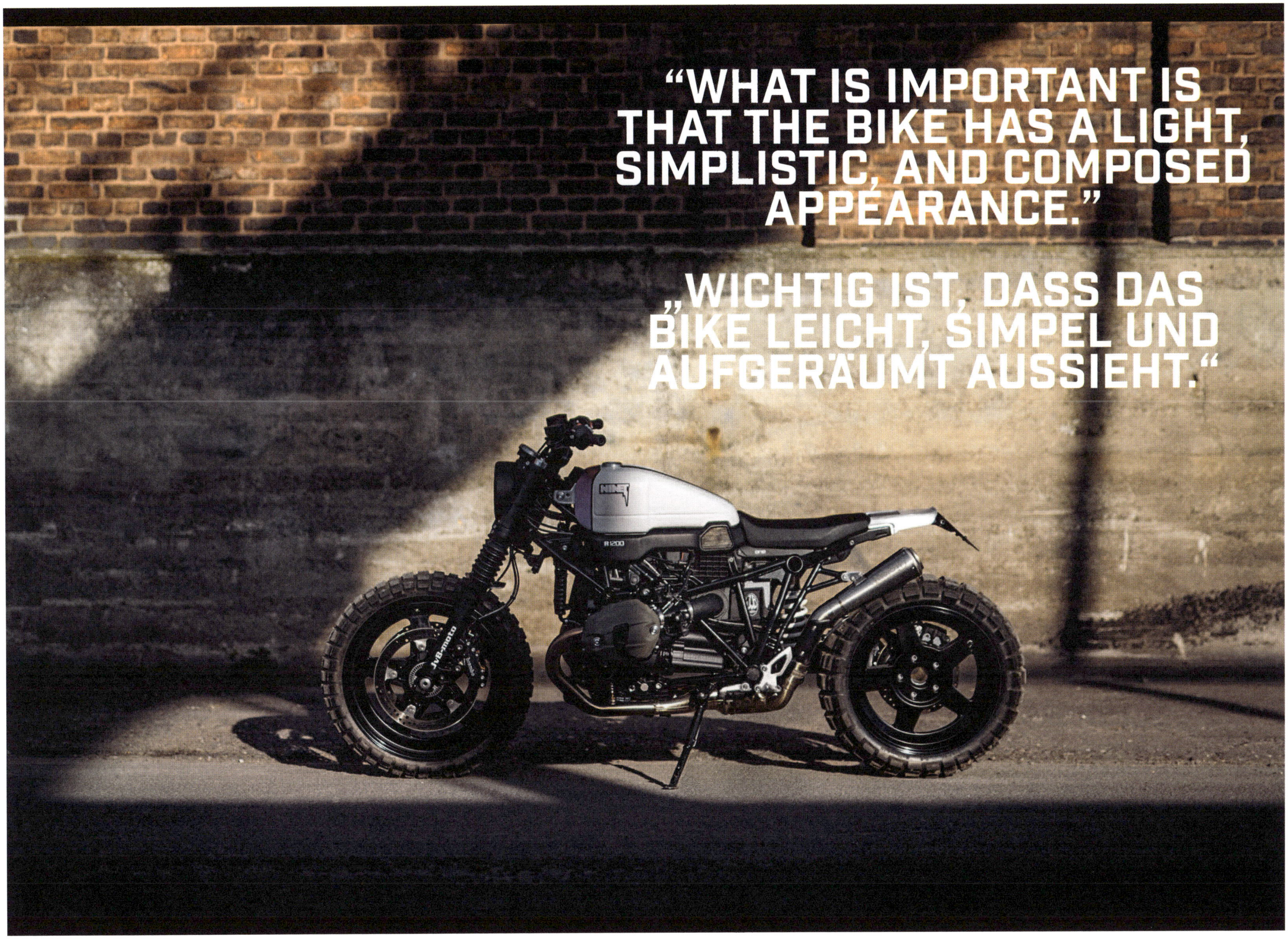
"WHAT IS IMPORTANT IS THAT THE BIKE HAS A LIGHT, SIMPLISTIC, AND COMPOSED APPEARANCE."
„WICHTIG IST, DASS DAS BIKE LEICHT, SIMPEL UND AUFGERÄUMT AUSSIEHT."

“PERFORMANCE AND APPEARANCE THEN GO HAND IN HAND.”

„PERFORMANCE UND OPTIK GEHEN DANN HAND IN HAND.“

"What is important is that the bike has a light, simplistic, and composed appearance," says Jens, simulating waves with hand movements. In doing so, the greatest challenge was the small fuel tank. "There's a whole lot of hullabaloo underneath," he says with a hint of Cologne dialect. "To hide all the electronic parts, I designed the ten-liter tank around them." In addition to the more streamlined appearance, the shorter tank has allowed the seat position to be significantly moved forward. The shifted center of gravity is particularly advantageous for an off-road bike. Jens knows this all too well. After all, the BMW is not the first scrambler made by JvB Moto. He thus outfitted the wheels with carbon shields, gave the exhaust manifold an ascending line, and installed an Arrow silencer.

The result of the custom treatment weighs in at a lean 196 kilograms. Everything about the vom Brauck interpretation of the scrambler is stripped down and streamlined. "I always try to leave a lot out. Performance and appearance then go hand in hand." However, the 1200 has not only become a compact motorcycle with a huge boxer engine, but has the professional aura of a serial production bike. It just seems more compact, more dynamic, and somehow extremely laid-back.

„Wichtig ist, dass das Bike leicht, simpel und aufgeräumt aussieht." Dazu macht Jens eine wellenförmige Handbewegung. Dabei war die größte Herausforderung der kleine Benzintank. „Da ist ganz schön viel Gedöns drunter", erzählt er mit kölschem Unterton. „Um alle Elektronikbauteile verstecken zu können, habe ich den Zehn-Liter-Tank drumrum konstruiert." Neben der schlankeren Optik ist die Sitzposition durch den kürzeren Tank nun deutlich nach vorne gerückt. Der verlagerte Schwerpunkt ist gerade für ein Offroad-Bike von Vorteil. Jens weiß das nur zu gut. Schließlich ist die BMW nicht der erste Scrambler aus dem Hause JvB Moto. Also verkleidete er die Räder mit Carbonblenden, er versah die Krümmeranlage mit einer ansteigenden Linie und montierte einen Arrow-Schalldämpfer.

Schlanke 196 Kilo sind das Ergebnis der Custom-Kur. Alles an der „vom-Brauck-Interpretation" des Scramblers wirkt reduziert und klar gegliedert. „Ich versuche immer, viel wegzulassen. Performance und Optik gehen dann Hand in Hand." Doch die 1200er ist nicht nur ein kompaktes Motorrad mit riesigem Boxer-Motor geworden; sie hat auch die professionelle Ausstrahlung eines Serienbikes. Nur dass sie kompakter, dynamischer und irgendwie sehr lässig wirkt.

1.2 R9T
S.E.V. MARCHAL

Hell On Wheels

HELL ON WHEELS MC
R NINE T SCRAMBLER

CUSTOMIZER	HELL ON WHEELS
ESTABLISHED	1993
LOCATED	SANTA ANA, CA, USA
INFO	HTTPS://HELLONWHEELSMC.COM

HELL ON WHEELS MC
R NINE T SCRAMBLER

Anyone who loves enduro riding and scrambling is sure to feel right at home in California. The landscapes are gorgeous, many areas are sparsely populated, and the spirit of the off-road riding tradition hovers in the air. No one knows this better than Hayden Roberts, who operates a workshop for classic dirt bikes and vintage British bikes called Hello Engine.

BMW Motorrad took notice of Hayden while shooting a video for the R nineT Scrambler. While filming was still in progress, they agreed that Hayden ought to get a chance to convert a scrambler and take part in the Soul Fuel project. In the meantime, Hayden fell in love with a woman named Joy Lewis, a cheerful blonde who was also working on set to help produce the film. Joy has remained by his side ever since. The two recently got married.

When asked whether the custom Scrambler was an instance of a Hell on Wheels MC or a Hello Engine custom bike, Joy paused to think for a bit and said, "When Hayden was helping out with the video clip for BMW Motorrad and the Soul Fuel deal was being discussed, he was a partner of the motorcycle workshop Hell on Wheels in Long Beach. Shortly afterward, he split from his partner and founded his own company."

Since Hayden almost exclusively restores and maintains classic motorcycles, the old-school tinkerer had to take some time to familiarize himself with the electrics of the modern four-valve engine: "The better I got to know the engine, the more I came to appreciate how non-complex it all worked. Every detail is well thought-out and the parts engage with one another." Weight reduction is part of Hayden's customizing philosophy, which means the BMW had to shed a few pounds: A short rear fender replaces the series fender, two compact mufflers run along one side, just below the flat seat.

Joy and Hayden agreed early on that the Boxer BMW should be converted into an old-school bike with a '70s style. The kind of jovial vehicle that makes you want to wear bell-bottoms, put on a few gold chains, and grow out a mustache. Both the rectangular Marchal fog lights and the custom-made throttle body housing are throwbacks to sports cars of a flashier era. More than anything else, the aims of these style-aware Californians are made clear once one takes a look at their color selection. "As with any

HELL ON WHEELS MC
R NINE T SCRAMBLER

Hell On Wheels

Wer Spaß an Enduro-Fahren und Scrambling hat, für den gibt es kaum einen besseren Ort als Kalifornien. Die Landschaften sind traumhaft schön, viele Gebiete kaum besiedelt und über allem schwebt eine lange Offroad-Tradition. Das weiß auch Hayden Roberts, der mittlerweile in Ventura seine Werkstatt für klassische Geländemotorräder und Vintage British Bikes mit dem Namen Hello Engine betreibt.

BMW Motorrad wurde bei einem Shooting für die R nineT Scrambler auf Hayden aufmerksam. Noch während der Dreharbeiten verabredeten sie, dass er eine Scrambler zum Umbauen erhalten und Teilnehmer des Soul Fuel Projekts werden solle. Und ganz nebenbei verliebte sich Hayden bei der Arbeit am Set in Joy Lewis, die ebenfalls beim Filmdreh mitwirkte. Seither begleitet ihn die stets gutgelaunte Blondine – erst kürzlich haben die beiden geheiratet.

Auf die Frage, ob es sich bei der Custom-Scrambler um einen Umbau von Hell on Wheels MC oder Hello Engine handelt, muss Joy kurz überlegen: „Als Hayden beim Clip für BMW Motorrad mitwirkte und der Soul Fuel Deal verabredet wurde, war er Teilhaber der Motorradwerkstatt Hell on Wheels in Long Beach. Kurz darauf trennte er sich von seinem Partner und gründete seine eigene Firma."

Da Hayden eigentlich fast ausschließlich klassische Motorräder restauriert und wartet, musste sich der Schrauber alten Schlages erst einmal an die Elektronik des modernen Vierventilers gewöhnen: „Ich habe mich mehr und mehr reingefunden und gemerkt, wie einfach alles funktioniert. Jedes Detail ist durchdacht und die Teile greifen ineinander." Da Gewichtsreduktion zu Haydens Customizing-Philosophie zählt, verlor auch die BMW einige Pfunde: Ein kurzer Heckfender ersetzt das Serienschutzblech, zwei kompakte Schalldämpfer verlaufen einseitig, knapp unterhalb der flachen Sitzbank.

Joy und Hayden waren sich schnell einig, dass aus dem Boxer ein Old-School-Bike im Stil der 70er-Jahre werden sollte. Ein fröhliches Gefährt, zu dem man am liebsten Schlaghose, Goldkettchen und Oberlippenbart tragen möchte. Sowohl die rechteckigen Marchal-Nebelscheinwerfer als auch selbstgefertigte Cover zum Schutz der Drosselklappengehäuse erinnern an Sportwagen jener schrillen Ära. Vor allem bei der Farbwahl lassen sich die Absichten der stilbewussten Kalifornier erkennen: „Wie bei

Husqvarna
“WHEN I’M RIDING A MOTORCYCLE, MY HEAD IS COMPLETELY CLEAR.”
„WENN ICH MOTORRAD FAHRE, IST MEIN KOPF VÖLLIG FREI.“

"EVERY DETAIL IS WELL THOUGHT-OUT AND THE PARTS ENGAGE WITH ONE ANOTHER."

„JEDES DETAIL IST DURCHDACHT UND DIE TEILE GREIFEN INEINANDER."

R9T

project, the most difficult part ends up being the paint," says Hayden. "How bright am I gonna make this one?"

Ultimately, the customizer was inspired by the BMW sports cars from the '70s. He decided to paint the bike in Ceylon Gold with black stripes. In conjunction with the plaid cloth seat, the stripes are a throwback to classic BMW models like the 3.0 CS E9-Coupé or the 2002. Joy, on the other hand, took responsibility for the second color scheme being used. She insisted on the bright white exhaust as well as the black and white stripes on the headlight housing and the bottom side of the fender.

However, Hayden Roberts didn't convert this BMW into a show bike. He always intended to ride it like it was going out of style. "I flew to Germany and my wife jumped on it, and then we rode it across Europe," he says, highlighting how much the bike can handle. "In principle, it's pretty easy to find the important things in life that make you truly happy. When I'm riding a motorcycle, my head is completely clear. That's what I like most about it. It's all about hearing the sound of the engine and finding the best stretch of road. One curve at a time."

jedem Projekt war auch hier die Festlegung auf einen Farbton sehr schwierig", erzählt Hayden. „Wie leuchtend und farbenfroh sollte die R nineT werden?"

Letztendlich haben den Customizer die BMW Sportwagen der Siebziger inspiriert. Er entschied sich für eine Lackierung in Ceylon Gold mit schwarzen Streifen. Gemeinsam mit der karierten Stoffsitzbank erinnert der Look an die klassischen BMW Modelle wie das 3.0 CS E9 Coupé oder den 2002. Joy hingegen zeichnet verantwortlich für das zweite verwendete Farbschema. Sie bestand auf den strahlend weißen Auspuff und die schwarz-weißen Streifen an Scheinwerfergehäuse und Schutzblechunterseite.

Doch Hayden Roberts hat die BMW nicht etwa als Showobjekt aufgebaut, sondern um sie ausgiebig zu fahren. „Wir sind nach Deutschland geflogen, meine Frau hat auf dem Soziussitz Platz genommen und so haben wir ganz Europa bereist", schwärmt er von den universellen Talenten der Maschine. „Es ist im Prinzip ganz einfach, die wichtigen Dinge im Leben zu finden, die einen wirklich glücklich machen. Wenn ich Motorrad fahre, ist mein Kopf völlig frei – das mag ich am meisten daran. Es geht dann nur noch um den Klang des Motors und darum, die beste Strecke zu finden. Kurve für Kurve."

Poets of Sprint
101
SPRINT-CREW
GLEMSECK 101
1.2 R9T

Rninet
Scrambler

HEIWA MOTORCYCLE
R NINE T SCRAMBLER

CUSTOMIZER	HEIWA MOTORCYCLE
ESTABLISHED	2005
LOCATED	HIROSHIMA, JAPAN
INFO	WWW.HEIWA-MC.JP

HEIWA MOTORCYCLE
R NINE T SCRAMBLER

Kengo Kimura actually specializes in customizing classic motorcycles. Old British bikes, US bikes, and Japanese bikes from the '70s. This means that the Scrambler conversion of the R nineT was the first time that the head of Heiwa, a renowned bike building company, has worked with a boxer engine. It is also unusual for Kengo to be redesigning a brand-new bike. "I had never worked on a BMW before. So I started by riding it—to work, into the city, and on trips—in order to familiarize myself with its characteristics," says Kengo. "At first something felt 'off' about the strong presence of the engine. But it's much easier to handle than it appears. The engine has a flat torque curve, and it's surprisingly light. It is simply easy to ride: I had no problem keeping up with friends who ride four-cylinder Japanese bikes."

The bike builder from Hiroshima quickly came to the conclusion that the BMW had to remain a motorcycle fit for active riding and with a lot of practical value. "We would usually build one show bike per year and pour all of our knowledge into it. However, these exceptional motorcycles are not very well-suited for daily riding," says Kengo, making his hand into a fist, "But here, it's about performance, too." He began working on the bike in September of 2016 with the goal in mind of creating a typical Heiwa bike without watering down the qualities of the series bike.

Although he didn't want to get too carried away for the sake of preserving the riding characteristics, Kengo still made significant modifications to the R nineT's components. "We changed two-thirds of the frame!" he recounts. For the Heiwa team, this meant redesigning both the rear frame and the main frame in order to obtain a straight line underneath the tank and seat. The idea was to install a fuel tank that was much narrower than the bulky series part, which would usually cover up that area of the frame. Since the redesigned aluminum tank turned out very small, Kengo designed an additional tank that guarantees a practical range and is tucked away neatly under

HEIWA MOTORCYCLE
R NINE T SCRAMBLER

Eigentlich hat sich Kengo Kimura auf das Customizing klassischer Motorräder spezialisiert. Auf alte Engländer, auf US-Bikes und auf Japaner der 1970er-Jahre. So ist der Scrambler-Umbau der R nineT nicht nur Boxer-Premiere für den Chef der Edelschmiede Heiwa, auch das Umgestalten eines fabrikneuen Motorrads ist ungewöhnlich für den Japaner. „Ich hatte zuvor nie an einer BMW gearbeitet. Also fuhr ich die R nineT Scrambler erst einmal – zur Arbeit, in die Stadt und auf Touren – um mich mit ihrem Charakter vertraut zu machen", erklärt Kengo. „Am Anfang hatte ich Respekt vor der starken Präsenz des Boxermotors. Aber die Scrambler fährt sich viel einfacher, als ich vermutete. Sie ist überraschend leicht und der Motor verfügt über eine angenehm flache Drehmomentkurve. Ich hatte keinerlei Probleme, meinen Freunden auf ihren japanischen Vierzylinder-Bikes zu folgen."

Schnell stand für den Schrauber aus Hiroshima fest, dass die BMW auch nach dem Umbau ein fahraktives Motorrad mit hohem Gebrauchswert bleiben sollte. „Normalerweise bauen wir ein Showbike pro Jahr, in das wir all unser Können stecken. Doch diese extremen Motorräder eignen sich nicht zum täglichen Fahren." Kengo ballt die Hand zur Faust: „Aber hier geht es auch um Performance!" Das Ziel vor Augen, ein typisches Heiwa-Bike entstehen zu lassen, ohne die dynamischen Qualitäten des Serienbikes zu verwässern, begann er im September 2016 mit der Arbeit.

Auch wenn er zugunsten des Fahrverhaltens nicht so sehr ins Extreme gehen wollte, modifizierte Kengo dennoch wesentliche Bauteile der R nineT. „Wir haben zwei Drittel des Rahmens geändert", erzählt er. So konstruierte das Heiwa-Team nicht nur den Heckrahmen neu, sondern auch den Hauptrahmen, um eine gerade Linie unter Tank und Sitzbank zu erhalten. Denn es sollte ein wesentlich schmalerer Benzintank als das bauchige Serienteil verbaut werden, das den Rahmen an dieser Stelle üblicherweise verdeckt. Weil der neu gestaltete Aluminiumtank sehr klein ausfällt, konstruierte

“IT IS ABOUT PERFORMANCE”

„HIER GEHT ES UM PERFORMANCE“

CUSTOM WORK SHOP
HEIWA
MOTOR CYCLE

“REGULAR CUSTOMERS WHO SAW THE FINISHED BIKE COMMENTED ON HOW IT HAS THE SIGNATURE HEIWA LOOK.”

the seat. He also installed the fuel pump needed for the fuel injection system here. For reasons of space, the airbox had to be scrapped to make room for a smaller custom-developed version. This new airbox, combined with the 2-into-2 exhaust system, allowed the bike builder to achieve a noticeably lower visual focal point. A discreet coat of beige paint over the frame and body parts also helps to bring out the desired vintage appearance.

For the wheels, the head of Heiwa opted for a BMW Motorrad product. He used the cross spoke wheel of the GS models. The aluminum protective plates of the classic-looking wheels are hand-made, just like the ribbed leather seat and the narrow handlebars. The unusual, vertically arranged front headlight and the mini rear light were taken from the Heiwa product range. When asked whether he is pleased with his Scrambler interpretation, Kengo replied calmly by saying, “Regular customers who saw the finished bike commented on how it has the signature Heiwa look. I personally don’t know which parts have our signature look—but I’ve done my best to create lines that I think look cool.”

Kengo einen Zusatztank, der eine praxisnahe Reichweite garantiert und geschickt unter dem Sattel versteckt ist. Hier montierte er auch die Benzinpumpe, die für die Einspritzanlage benötigt wird. Aus Platzgründen musste die Airbox einer kleineren, selbst entwickelten Version weichen. In Verbindung mit der parallel angeordneten 2-in-2-Auspuffanlage erreichte der Bike-Builder so eine spürbare Absenkung des optischen Schwerpunkts. Eine schlichte Lackierung von Rahmen und Bodyparts in Beige unterstützt darüber hinaus die gewünschte Vintage-Optik.

Bei den Rädern griff der Heiwa-Chef ins Regal von BMW Motorrad – er verwendete die Kreuzspeichenräder der GS Modelle. Die Schutzbleche aus Aluminiumblech über den klassisch aussehenden Rädern sind handgearbeitet, ebenso wie der gerippte Ledersattel und der schmale Rohrlenker. Der ungewöhnliche, vertikal angeordnete Frontscheinwerfer und das Mini-Rücklicht stammen aus dem Heiwa-Programm. Auf die Frage, ob er mit seiner Scrambler-Interpretation zufrieden sei, antwortet Kengo bescheiden: „Meine Kunden sagen, die R nineT habe den typischen Heiwa-Look. Ich habe mein Bestes gegeben, Formen zu finden, die cool aussehen.“

ABS
TRIP
INFO

SOSA METALWORKS
SMW 61-B

CUSTOMIZER	SOSA METALWORKS
ESTABLISHED	2012
LOCATED	LAS VEGAS, NV, USA
INFO	WWW.SOSAMETALWORKS.COM

SOSA METALWORKS
SMW 61-B

"Mastering a skill is not about having the best tools. It's about making the best of the tools you have." Cristian Sosa startles his trainees by opening his speech with this bit of knowledge. They have traveled from all over the world to attend one of his metal shaping and design classes. "I try to eliminate the excuse about 'I can't do this kind of work because I don't have this or that piece of equipment.' Working with your hands is always an option," says Sosa with a serious expression. "Doing a lot with a little", however, is not this American's sole philosophy. Sosa expects those attending his course to work ideas out on their own using just their intellect before even thinking about picking up a hammer and sandbag.

However, we wouldn't even be talking about this full-bearded "metal sculptor" if his singular reputation were that of a teacher and trainer. As a matter of fact, Cristian Sosa has also been running Sosa Metalworks in Las Vegas in company with his brother Roberto since 2012. There, he devotes most of his work to creating original motorcycle transformations. The main focus of attention of this work is unequivocally placed on conceptual design and creation of metal bodywork—gas tanks, covers, and racing seats made from aluminum or steel sheet. There can be no doubt that the custom bikes from Sosa Metalworks have earned the small workshop a place among the custom builders of the next generation. The bikes aren't just fearlessly designed and built to artisanal perfection. They are miles beyond anything resembling stale and ostentatious "biker" products. The BMW R nineT, which BMW Motorrad handed over to the Sosa brothers in early 2017, is itself equivalent to such high criteria. What they had in mind was creating something absolutely one-of-a-kind without watering down the distinctiveness of the original. The duo wanted to sharpen the design while leaving the spirit of the boxer intact. And the idea was to make this all happen by hand using simple tools—keeping with the Sosa tradition.

The Sosa crew built the curved tank/seat profile of the SMW 61-B, as the creation came to be known, as a single piece of aluminum monocoque with a pronounced

SOSA METALWORKS
SMW 61-B

„Beim Bewältigen einer Aufgabe ist es nicht wichtig, die besten Werkzeuge zu haben. Vielmehr geht es darum, aus den vorhandenen Mitteln das Beste zu machen." Mit dieser Weisheit überrascht Cristian Sosa seine Lehrlinge, die aus der ganzen Welt anreisen, um einen seiner Kurse der „Metalshaping and Design Classes" zu besuchen. „Ich akzeptiere keine Ausreden, wenn mal das passende Equipment fehlt. Handarbeit ist immer eine Option", sagt Sosa mit strengem Blick. „Aus wenig viel machen", ist aber nicht die einzige Philosophie des US-Amerikaners. So erwartet Sosa von den Kursteilnehmern seiner Metall-Workshops, ihren Verstand einzusetzen und eigene Ideen zu entwickeln, bevor es mit Hammer und Sandsack an die Arbeit geht.

Doch wir würden an dieser Stelle kaum über den vollbärtigen Blechkünstler sprechen, wenn er ausschließlich als Lehrer und Ausbilder in Erscheinung getreten wäre. Cristian Sosa betreibt darüber hinaus seit 2012 mit seinem Bruder Roberto die Firma Sosa Metalworks in Las Vegas, wo er sich vor allem der kreativen Umgestaltung von Motorrädern widmet. Das Hauptaugenmerk liegt dabei eindeutig auf dem Entwurf und der Herstellung von metallenem Bodywork – Tanks, Verkleidungen und Höckersitzbänke aus Aluminium oder Stahlblech. Die Custombikes von Sosa Metalworks ordnen die kleine Manufaktur eindeutig ein in die Schublade „Next Generation Custom Builders". Sie sind nicht nur mutig gestaltet und handwerklich perfekt ausgeführt, sie haben sich auch meilenweit entfernt von miefigem Biker-Kitsch. Auch die BMW R nineT, die BMW Motorrad Anfang 2017 in die Hände der Sosa-Brüder gegeben hat, entspricht diesen Kriterien. Ihnen schwebte vor, etwas Einzigartiges zu erschaffen, ohne die markante Basis zu verwässern. Die beiden wollten das Design anschärfen, aber die Seele des Boxers erhalten. Und das alles sollte – ganz nach Sosa-Tradition – mit einfachen Mitteln und von Hand entstehen.

Die geschwungene Tank-Sitzbank-Linie der SMW 61-B hat die Sosa-Crew als einteiliges Aluminium-Monocoque mit ausgeprägter Mittelnaht angefertigt. Über das extrem kurze Heck schmiegt sich ein knappes, dunkelrotes Echtlederpolster. An den Radien

“DOING A LOT WITH A LITTLE”

„AUS WENIG VIEL MACHEN“

“WORKING WITH YOUR HANDS IS ALWAYS AN OPTION.”

„HANDARBEIT IST IMMER EINE OPTION.“

middle seam. The extremely short rear end is cushioned with taut, dark-red leather. The primary feature placing the design in a class of its own is the sleek full fairing, which has been meticulously hammered from a single sheet of aluminum and crafted to the specific curvature of the chassis parts. The aesthetics and striking curves as well as the decision to forego a fiberglass-reinforced windshield illuminate the fact that the bike builders would settle for no less than perfection in design and execution, especially for the metal parts.

Under the monocoque, the SMW 61-B remains remarkably similar to a standard R nineT. The drive unit, spoke wheels, chassis components and even the double exhaust installed on one side are all left over from the original bike and are being used in the SMW 61-B without any major modifications. Nevertheless, the machine runs like a thrilling one-off café racer, an elaborately styled retro sport bike—which speaks for the quality of the series parts. The Sosa brothers' work of art gets most of its distinctive charm from the artfully crafted aluminum sheeting parts, reaffirming the credo of these two craftsman: "Doing a lot with a little."

der Karosserieteile orientiert sich auch die schlanke, sorgfältig aus einer Aluminiumtafel gehämmerte Vollverkleidung, die vorrangig für das ungewöhnliche Design verantwortlich ist. Ihre sinnliche und schwungvolle Formgebung sowie der Verzicht auf eine GfK-Scheibe verdeutlichen den Anspruch von Perfektion bei Gestaltung und Ausführung vor allem der Metallteile.

Unter dem Monocoque ist die SMW 61-B eine erstaunlich seriennahe R nineT geblieben. Antriebseinheit, Speichenräder, Fahrwerkskomponenten und sogar der einseitig verlegte Doppelauspuff entstammen dem Basisbike und wurden ohne größere Änderungen weiterverwendet. Dennoch wirkt die Maschine wie ein begehrenswertes Cafe-Racer-Unikat, ein aufwendig durchgestylter Retro-Sportler – was für die Qualität der Serienteile spricht. Ihren unverwechselbaren Charme bezieht Sosas Kreation vor allem aus den kunstvoll gearbeiteten Aluminiumblechteilen, ganz nach dem Credo des Meisters: „Mit wenig Aufwand viel erreichen".

BMW
brembo

PROTAPER
BMW
Gunn
DAN RILEY
32
BDMX

Gunn

GUNN DESIGN
R NINE T SCRAMBLER

CUSTOMIZER	GUNN DESIGN
ESTABLISHED	2008
LOCATED	BURNSVILLE, MN, USA
INFO	WWW.GUNNDESIGN.US

Gunn

GUNN DESIGN
R NINE T SCRAMBLER

Dan Riley is considered a prime example of a customizer from the "next generation." He's young, has an established style, and enjoys success working as a freelance graphic designer. At his studio, Gunn Design, he also ventures into the realm of professional two-wheeler conversion. "I've been fully committed to beautifying the world. And my world is motorcycles," says Dan with confidence. "I have built dozens of bikes over the years," says the American, illustrating that he knows what he's talking about. There's no doubt about it—he gives his bikes minimalist, dynamic, and well-proportioned designs.

BMW Motorrad was hoping that this creative mind from Burnsville, Minnesota would prove to be a lucky find. The Bavarians had chosen Gunn Design as a participant in the Soul Fuel project and provided Dan with a brand-new R nineT Scrambler to convert. He knew right away what he had to do. What he had in mind was a wiry sports bike in the style of the flat track racers that are highly popular in the USA. It could either be used as a breathtaking show bike or taken out to the sandy oval track and used as an actual racing bike. Dan smirks and says "I wanted to race it in the RSD Super Hooligan National Championship race series."

But first, the 1200cc bike had to be given a radical Gunn Design treatment. The goal was to make the boxer bike slimmer and noticeably lighter. So, Dan removed the standard bodywork and replaced it with a small fuel tank from a 400cc sports bike and a narrow-cut hump seat made of extremely lightweight carbon. The original wheels were swapped out for a combination of aluminum hubs from Woody's Wheelworks, sun rims, and spokes from Buchanan's. Dunlop DT-3 racing tires highlight the sophisticated standards of the bike builder. For improved road holding under extreme conditions, he installed a strut from Race Tech. Aluminum footpegs from Biltwell were added to ensure optimal contact with the bike. Last but not least, the head honcho at Gunn

GUNN DESIGN
R NINE T SCRAMBLER

Dan Riley gilt als Musterbeispiel für einen Customizer der Next Generation. Er ist jung, stilsicher und arbeitet erfolgreich als Freelance-Grafikdesigner. Mit seinem Studio Gunn Design wagt er sich zudem an die professionelle Umgestaltung von Zweirädern. „Ich betrachte es als meine Aufgabe, die Welt zu verschönern. Und meine Welt sind nun mal Motorräder", sagt Dan selbstbewusst. „Über die Jahre habe ich Dutzende von Bikes aufgebaut", untermauert der US-Amerikaner seine markigen Aussagen mit soliden Fakten. Keine Frage, seine Bikes gestaltet er minimalistisch, dynamisch und überaus wohlproportioniert.

Für BMW Motorrad sollte sich der kreative Kopf aus Burnsville im Bundesstaat Minnesota als wahrer Glücksgriff erweisen. Die Bayern hatten Gunn Design als Teilnehmer für das Projekt Soul Fuel auserkoren und Dan eine nagelneue R nineT Scrambler zum Umbauen geliefert. Er wusste sofort, was zu tun war. Ihm schwebte ein drahtiges Sportbike im Stil der in den USA beliebten Flat-Track-Racer vor, das sich nicht nur als atemberaubendes Showbike anbietet, sondern auch Einsätze auf dem sandigen Oval einer Flat-Track-Rennstrecke erlaubt. Dan grinst: „Ich habe mir in den Kopf gesetzt, mit der BMW an der ‚RSD Super Hooligan National Championship' teilzunehmen."

Doch zunächst musste die 1200er einer radikalen Gunn Design-Kur unterzogen werden. Das Boxer-Bike sollte schlanker und spürbar leichter werden. Also entfernte Dan das serienmäßige Bodywork und ersetzte es durch den kleinen Benzintank eines 400-ccm-Supersportlers und eine knapp geschnittene Höckersitzbank aus federleichtem Carbon. Die originalen Räder tauschte er gegen eine Kombination aus Aluminiumnaben von Woody's Wheel Works, Sun-Felgen und Speichen von Buchanan's. Dunlop-DT3-Rennreifen unterstreichen den seriösen Anspruch des Bike-Builders. Für verbesserte Straßenlage im Extrembereich verbaute er ein Federbein von Race-Tech, optimalen Kontakt zum Motorrad ermöglichen Alufußrasten von Biltwell. Zu guter

“I’VE BEEN FULLY COMMITTED TO BEAUTI-FYING THE WORLD.”

„ICH BETRACHTE ES ALS MEINE AUFGABE, DIE WELT ZU VERSCHÖNERN.“

brembo
DUNLOP

32
DAN RILEY

32
DUNLOP
DUNLOP

Gunn

created an elevated two-into-two titanium exhaust system with a striking bend, helping to further reduce the weight of an already very light BMW.

When the finished Soul Fuel BMW appeared in the Old Iron /Young Blood bike show at the Buffalo Chip venue during the Sturgis Rally of August 2017, Dan felt a sense of satisfaction from having so easily achieved his first milestone: His minimalistic creation stood out exceptionally well among brilliant show bikes from Arlen Ness, Perewitz Cycle Fabrication, Hazan Motorworks, and Klock Werks.

Shortly afterward, Dan fulfilled a dream of his: He attached starting numbers, slipped on his full-face helmet and rode the BMW around the dusty oval in three Super Hooligan races. Sturgis, Wheels and Waves California, and The See See, he says with pride. Street bike flat track racing lets him show off the fact that his R nineT can do a lot more than just look pretty...

Letzt fertigte Dan in seiner Werkstatt eine hochgelegte 2-in-2-Titanauspuffanlage mit kühnem Krümmerschwung an, die ebenfalls dazu beiträgt, die Pfunde der ohnehin nicht besonders schweren BMW weiter zu senken.

Als die fertige Soul Fuel BMW im August 2017 im Rahmen des Buffalo Chip in Sturgis auf der Bikeshow Old Iron/Young Blood steht, stellt Dan mit Genugtuung fest, dass er sein erstes Etappenziel locker erreicht hat: Zwischen glänzenden Showbikes von Arlen Ness, Perewitz Cycle Fabrication, Hazan Motorworks oder Klock Werks macht sich seine minimalistische Kreation ausgesprochen gut.

Kurz darauf erfüllt sich Dan einen Traum: Er bringt Startnummern an, streift den Integralhelm über und treibt die BMW bei drei Super-Hooligan-Rennen über das staubige Oval. Sturgis, Wheels and Waves California und The See See, zählt er stolz auf. Denn beim Street Bike Flat Track Racing kann er beweisen, dass seine R nineT viel mehr kann, als nur gut aussehen ...

THE AUTHOR Dirk Mangartz has been working as a motor journalist for various book and magazine publishers since 1992. He was the editor-in-chief of the motorcycle magazine *Custombike* for 15 years. Today he writes texts about motor vehicles for magazines and daily newspapers such as *Fuel* (Motorpresse), *Craftrad*, *Kustom Life Magazine* or the *Hamburger Abendblatt*. His latest book publications include *The Harley-Davidson Book* and *Custom Bike Life*, which were released by teNeues in 2017, as well as *Moto Guzzi California* (Delius Klasing, 2018).

DER AUTOR Dirk Mangartz arbeitet seit 1992 als Motorjournalist für verschiedene Buch- und Zeitschriftenverlage. Er war 15 Jahre lang als Chefredakteur für das Motorradmagazin *Custombike* tätig. Heute verfasst er Texte zu Kraftfahrzeugthemen für Magazine und Tageszeitungen wie *Fuel* (Motorpresse), *Craftrad*, *Kustom Life Magazine* oder das *Hamburger Abendblatt*. Zu seinen letzten Buchpublikationen zählen *The Harley-Davidson Book* und *Custom Bike Life*, die 2017 bei teNeues erschienen sind, sowie *Moto Guzzi California* (Delius Klasing, 2018).

Thank you

Thanks to all those who contributed to this book: those who drafted, designed, wrote, edited, translated, and supervised. Special thanks to those who contributed the photos that gave us exceptional insight into both the bigger picture and the many small details of these wonderful machines and their builders. And, in particular, thanks to the 17 customizers, who have given wings to our imagination and fueled our souls with their R nineT customizations. You and the entire customizer scene continue to inspire the motorcycle world due to your creativity and craftsmanship.

Ein Dank geht an alle, die an diesem Buch mitgewirkt haben: die gestaltet, getextet, konzipiert, lektoriert, übersetzt und überwacht haben. Besonders sei denen gedankt, die uns mit ihren Fotografien einen einzigartigen Blick auf die wunderbaren Maschinen und ihre Erbauer, auf das große Ganze und auf viele kleine Details gewähren. Und vor allem den 17 Customizern, die mit ihren Überarbeitungen der R nineT unsere Fantasie beflügeln und Treibstoff für die Seele liefern. Sie und die ganze Customizerszene versorgen die Motorradwelt dank ihrer Kreativität und Handwerkskunst permanent mit Inspiration.

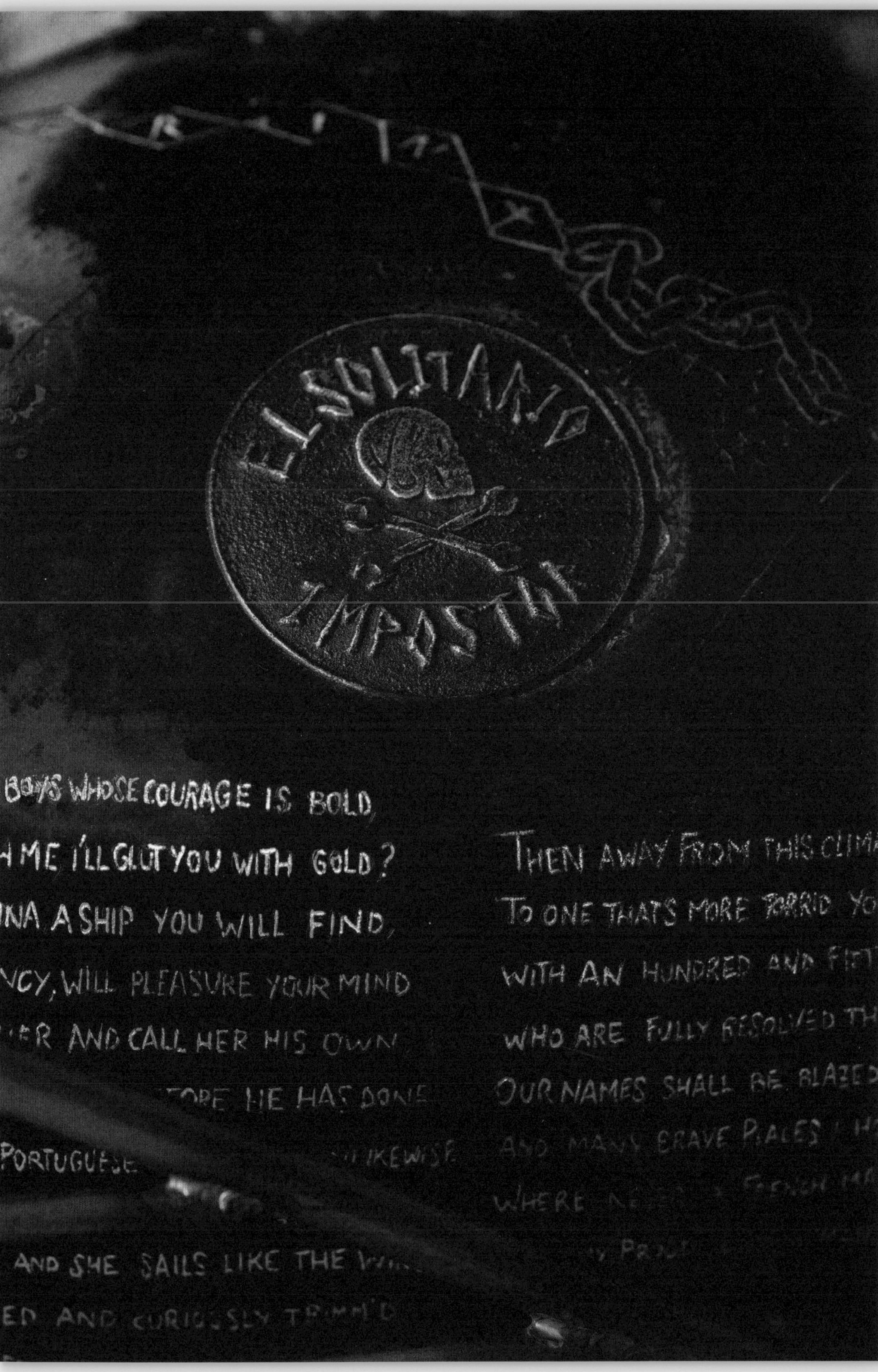

CREDITS

p. 2: © Markus Hofman
p. 5: © Michael Lichter
pp. 6/7: © Amy Shore
p. 9: © Laurent Nivalle
p. 11: © BMW AG
p. 12: © Markus Hofman
p. 15: © BMW AG
pp. 16/17: © BMW AG
p. 19: © Adam Fedderly
p. 21, left: © Adam Fedderly
p. 21, top right, bottom right: © BMW AG
pp. 22/23: © Adam Fedderly
p. 24, top left: © Uwe Fischer
p. 24, bottom right: © Adam Fedderly
p. 25: © Uwe Fischer
p. 26: © Tim Adler
p. 29: © Tobias Schult Photography
pp. 30–33: © Tim Adler
p. 33, bottom right: © BMW AG
p. 34: © Iker Basterretxea
p. 37, left: © David Borras
p. 37, right: © Markus Hofman
p. 38, left: © Iker Basterretxea
p. 38, right: © William Anthony
p. 40, top left: © Iker Basterretxea
p. 40, bottom left, top right, and bottom right: © William Anthony
p. 41: © Iker Basterretxea
p. 43: © Laurent Nivalle
p. 44: © Laurent Nivalle
pp. 46/47: © Markus Hofman
pp. 48/49: © Laurent Nivalle
pp. 51–57: © Markus Hofman
pp. 59–65: © Jenny Jurnelius
pp. 66–101: © Ken Takayanagi
p. 102: © JL Photography
p. 104: © Simone De Ranieri
pp. 106–109: © JL Photography
pp. 110–117: © Michael Lichter
pp. 119–123: © Victor Jon Goico
p. 124: © Kristina Fender
p. 126: © Kristina Fender
p. 129: © Stephan Vens
pp. 130–133: © Kristina Fender
pp. 134–141: © Hiromitsu Yasui
pp. 142–156: © Michael Lichter, except p. 153, left: © Rudolf Bekker
p. 158: © Dirk Mangartz
p. 159: © Iker Basterretxea

For latest updates on the Soul Fuel project please visit:
www.bmw-motorrad.com/custom

Aktuelle Informationen zum Soul Fuel Projekt gibt es unter:
www.bmw-motorrad.com/custom

IMPRINT

Foreword: Michael Lichter
Texts: Dirk Mangartz
Translations: STAR Software, Translation, Artwork, Recording GmbH
Copyediting: Andy Dukes (English) and Dr. Simone Bischoff (German)
Proofreading: Inga Wortmann and Nele Wüsten, teNeues Media
Concept and Project Management: Martin Bölt, Nathalie Geßler, Thrass Papadimitriou, and Christian Pingitzer, BMW Motorrad
Editorial Coordination: Pit Pauen, teNeues Media

Creative Director: Martin Graf, teNeues Media
Design: Anika Lethen
Production: Dieter Haberzettl, teNeues Media
Color separation: Robin Hopp, teNeues Media

ISBN 978-3-96171-051-5
Library of Congress Number: 2018904697

Printed in Italy

teNeues Publishing Group
Kempen
Berlin
London
Munich
New York
Paris

teNeues

Bibliographic information published by the Deutsche Nationalbibliothek
The Deutsche Nationalbibliothek lists this publication in the Deutsche Nationalbibliografie; detailed bibliographic data are available on the Internet at http://dnb.dnb.de.

Published by teNeues Publishing Group

teNeues Media GmbH & Co. KG
Am Selder 37, 47906 Kempen, Germany
Phone: +49-(0)2152-916-0
Fax: +49-(0)2152-916-111
e-mail: books@teneues.com

MIX
Paper from responsible sources
FSC® C084761
FSC www.fsc.org

Press department: Andrea Rehn
Phone: +49-(0)2152-916-202
e-mail: arehn@teneues.com

Munich Office
Pilotystraße 4, 80538 Munich, Germany
Phone: +49-(0)89-443-8889-62
e-mail: bkellner@teneues.com

Berlin Office
Kohlfurter Straße 41–43, 10999 Berlin, Germany
Phone: +49-(0)30-4195-3526-23
e-mail: ajasper@teneues.com

teNeues Publishing Company
350 7th Avenue, Suite 301, New York, NY 10001, USA
Phone: +1-212-627-9090
Fax: +1-212-627-9511

teNeues Publishing UK Ltd.
12 Ferndene Road, London SE24 0AQ, UK
Phone: +44-(0)20-3542-8997

teNeues France S.A.R.L.
39, rue des Billets, 18250 Henrichemont, France
Phone: +33-(0)2-4826-9348
Fax: +33-(0)1-7072-3482

www.teneues.com